Success for Our Youngest Learners

Embracing the PLC at Work® Process at the Early Childhood Level

Barbara W. Cirigliano

Copyright © 2020 by Solution Tree Press

Materials appearing here are copyrighted. With one exception, all rights are reserved. Readers may reproduce only those pages marked "Reproducible." Otherwise, no part of this book may be reproduced or transmitted in any form or by any means (electronic, photocopying, recording, or otherwise) without prior written permission of the publisher.

555 North Morton Street
Bloomington, IN 47404
800.733.6786 (toll free) / 812.336.7700
FAX: 812.336.7790

email: info@SolutionTree.com
SolutionTree.com

Visit **go.SolutionTree.com/PLCbooks** to download the free reproducibles in this book.

Printed in the United States of America

Library of Congress Cataloging-in-Publication Data

Names: Cirigliano, Barbara W., author.
Title: Success for our youngest learners : embracing the PLC at work process at the early childhood level / Barbara W. Cirigliano.
Description: Bloomington, IN : Solution Tree Press, 2020. | Includes bibliographical references and index.
Identifiers: LCCN 2020002266 (print) | LCCN 2020002267 (ebook) | ISBN 9781947604735 (paperback) | ISBN 9781947604742 (ebook)
Subjects: LCSH: Early childhood teachers--In-service training. | Early childhood teachers--Professional relationships. | Professional learning communities.
Classification: LCC LB1732.3 .C57 2020 (print) | LCC LB1732.3 (ebook) | DDC 372.21--dc23
LC record available at https://lccn.loc.gov/2020002266
LC ebook record available at https://lccn.loc.gov/2020002267

Solution Tree
Jeffrey C. Jones, CEO
Edmund M. Ackerman, President

Solution Tree Press
President and Publisher: Douglas M. Rife
Associate Publisher: Sarah Payne-Mills
Art Director: Rian Anderson
Managing Production Editor: Kendra Slayton
Production Editor: Miranda Addonizio
Content Development Specialist: Amy Rubenstein
Copy Editor: Kate St. Ives
Proofreader: Elisabeth Abrams
Text and Cover Designer: Kelsey Hergül
Editorial Assistants: Sarah Ludwig and Elijah Oates

ACKNOWLEDGMENTS

Ever since I was a little girl playing school in my basement, I wanted to teach young children. I was lucky enough to be able to do that for many years. In 1999, Kildeer District 96 opened an early childhood center and was in search of a principal—my dream job.

I want to thank Kildeer District 96 for giving me this incredible opportunity to be part of its amazing school district. It was where I was introduced to the Professional Learning Communities at Work concept and where I began the process of implementation in my school, Willow Grove Kindergarten and Early Childhood Center. I was extremely fortunate to work with great administrators, teachers, families, and kids in an area that I am passionate about—young children.

Thanks to Tom Many, who encouraged me to write (I hated it), and to Chris Jakicic, who got me started on writing this book. I am grateful to Claudia Wheatley, because every time she saw me, she encouraged me to write this book.

Most of all, I thank all those kids who gave me a reason to write this book. You are my heroes.

Solution Tree Press would like to thank the following reviewers:

Julie Gorvett
  Principal
  Early Learning Center
  Schaumburg, Illinois

Sarah Hall
  First-Grade Teacher
  Longwood Elementary School
  Longwood, Florida

Dana Huff
  Early Kindergarten Teacher
  Mountain Meadow Elementary School
  Buckley, Washington

JoAnna McIlory
  Deputy Principal
  Singapore American School
  Singapore

Carolyn Carter Miller
  Solution Tree Associate
  Fredericksburg, Virginia

Keri Van Vleet
  Kindergarten Teacher
  Tomé Elementary School
  Los Lunas, New Mexico

Visit **go.SolutionTree.com/PLCbooks** to download the free reproducibles in this book.

TABLE OF CONTENTS

ABOUT THE AUTHOR ix

INTRODUCTION 1
    PLCs and the Importance of Effective Early Childhood Programs 3
    The Challenges of Collaboration for Early Childhood Educators 5
    About This Book 6

Chapter 1
The Need for High-Quality Early Childhood Programs 9
    Outcomes for Students in Early Childhood Programs 10
    What Successful Teams in Early Childhood Programs Can Accomplish 14

Chapter 2
The Building Blocks of a PLC 21
    The Three Big Ideas of a PLC 22
    The Four Critical Questions of a PLC 24
    Collective Inquiry 25
    Action Research 27
    The Four Pillars of a PLC 28
        Mission 28
        Vision 31
        Values 32
        Goals 34
        How the Pillars Work Together 35

Chapter 3
Collaborative Teams in Early Childhood Programs 37

    Types of Teams 38
        Grade-Level Teams 38
        Vertical Teams 40
        Curriculum Teams 41
        Leadership Teams 41
        Problem-Solving Teams 42
    Organizing Teams 43
        Specialists on Teams 44
        Electronic Teams 45
    Collaborative Teams for Early Childhood Educators 47
        Making Time for Teams to Meet 50
        Focusing on the Right Things 51
        Using Team Tools 64

Chapter 4
A Focus on Learning 69

    A Shift From Teaching Students to Students Learning 69
    The Configurations of Early Childhood Classrooms 72
    What Is a Guaranteed and Viable Curriculum? 74
    The Need for Early Childhood Essential Standards 77
        What Do We Want Our Students to Know and Be Able to Do? 78
        A Protocol for Determining Essential Standards 80
            Step One 81
            Step Two 81
            Step Three 81
            Step Four 82
            Step Five 82
        How to Pace the Standards 84

Chapter 5
Assessment 87

    Why Assess Early Childhood Students? 89
    What Do Preschool and Kindergarten Assessments Look Like? 92
        Teacher Team–Created Assessments 92
            Checklists 94
            Anecdotal Notes 95
            Rubrics 98
        Purchased Early Childhood Assessments 99

Chapter 6
Data and Interventions **103**

    The Importance of Data 103
    How to Look at Data 105
    A Protocol for Reviewing Data..107
        Gather the Data 107
        Analyze the Data..107
        Plan a Response to the Data 108
        Reflect on the Assessment 109
    How to Provide Support Through Interventions 112

CONCLUSION **119**

REFERENCES AND RESOURCES **123**

INDEX **135**

ABOUT THE AUTHOR

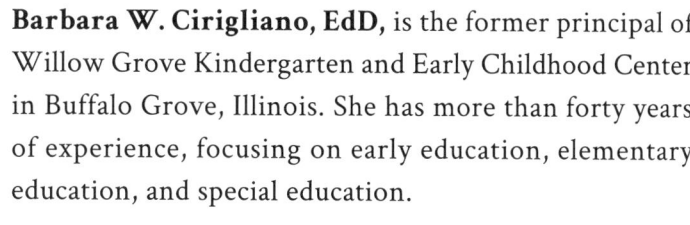

Barbara W. Cirigliano, EdD, is the former principal of Willow Grove Kindergarten and Early Childhood Center in Buffalo Grove, Illinois. She has more than forty years of experience, focusing on early education, elementary education, and special education.

At Willow Grove, Dr. Cirigliano led the implementation of a professional learning community. Along with her staff, she created a collaborative culture and developed a guaranteed and viable curriculum supported by the Common Core State Standards (CCSS). Their creation of common assessments and a pyramid of interventions has built the foundation for student learning in this high-performing district. The National Association for the Education of Young Children has accredited Willow Grove for the past several years. This rigorous accreditation process identifies high-quality early learning programs and schools. Willow Grove has also been highlighted on the AllThingsPLC website (https://allthingsplc.info).

Dr. Cirigliano has a bachelor's degree in early childhood special education, a master's degree in educational leadership, and a doctorate in educational administration. She has presented at a variety of national conferences.

To book Barbara W. Cirigliano for professional development, contact pd@SolutionTree.com.

INTRODUCTION

During my tenure as principal of an early childhood center, I encountered many educators of young children who believed that the professional learning community (PLC) process did not apply to them. However, the PLC process as articulated by Richard DuFour, Rebecca DuFour, Robert Eaker, Thomas W. Many, and Mike Mattos (2016) is a powerful way to ensure that all students learn at high levels. *All* should include the youngest students, too. As an educator of young children, you may not be included in the PLC conversations in your school. You may not yet be familiar with the basic premises of a PLC or understand yet how you can apply the concepts to yourself and your students. But this paradigm can and must shift. Your students are part of the *all*, and you need to be included in these important conversations and learning opportunities.

For seventeen years, I led Willow Grove Kindergarten and Early Childhood Center, part of Kildeer Countryside Community Consolidated School District 96 (KCSD 96) in Illinois, which has been recognized as a model PLC. Teachers from as far away as Australia and as close as next door visited our school district. They wanted to see teams meeting and collaborating, students learning, and the PLC process in action. Our visitors were always surprised that not only did we have an early childhood center but that it was part of our districtwide PLC. These visiting early childhood educators found it difficult to understand how they could apply the PLC process to their programs for young children. They had seen it work at the elementary level in their own school districts, but they believed early childhood education was different. While early childhood education has unique challenges and needs, the PLC process is the best way to meet these challenges and needs—I believe to the benefit of all. I was determined to let our wondering visitors know that extending the PLC process to the early childhood or preK level (that is, students aged three to five) could increase student learning and strengthen their own teaching skills. This book illustrates how to bring about a transformation in any early childhood program that will give it the capability to function as part of the school or district PLC.

The visiting preK teachers with whom I spoke over the years expressed hesitance to entertain the value of PLCs for early childhood education for a variety of reasons, but a reason that featured prominently in their hesitance again and again was their aversion to the idea of including assessment practices in the education of very young children—and assessment is always part of an effective PLC. They had this assumption that testing is just not for the preK level, that it's not a developmentally appropriate practice. These preK teachers did not really understand the power of assessments or how to design or administer them. If these teachers did assess, they did it at a student's entrance into their program, and often they did nothing with whatever results emerged from their version of assessment. They were unclear how to use data effectively in order to provide support and enrichment to their students. In fact, there are appropriate ways to assess young children that provide important data. I go into much more detail in chapter 5 (page 87).

I explained that, initially, Willow Grove teachers also avoided assessing students' learning, and, indeed, did not see the value in formalized assessment practices. Instead, each classroom teacher determined (in his or her own way) what skills each student in the class had achieved, and they reported their perspectives on assessment to parents at conference time. However, Willow Grove teachers came to realize that in order to commit fully to the PLC process, they needed to commit to engaging in thoughtful, formalized assessment and data analysis practices—with the young children they teach. I will explain more about this transition and using data to design interventions in early education in chapter 6 (page 103).

At Willow Grove, we began working together and functioning as a PLC in the early 2000s. We started small, with just a few assessments, but continued the journey every day, week, month, and year. I prompted the staff to start with assessments when I noticed that each preK teacher favored different learning skills. Some thought that students must be able to identify eight colors while others felt that only five were important. We started simply with color recognition just to see what information we could gather. We had to agree, as a team, what the most important colors were that we would all assess. We had to collaborate.

Our staff learned that collaborating to discuss student learning would provide students with the best education possible and the opportunity to achieve high levels of learning. We learned this along with our colleagues in every school in the district. We all began to see positive results in student achievement, and we all began to feel a positive energy as professionals. As an administrator, it was helpful for me to be able to discuss the PLC concept with my peers, just as it was for teachers.

Our experience at Willow Grove led me to write this book specifically for teachers of young children. Teacher leaders, school leadership teams, instructional coaches, and school administrators with early childhood programs as part of their schools may also find it useful. Information in this book will help central office staff understand how important it is that PLCs include all programs in their school districts.

I know that preK teachers believe in the power of high-quality early childhood education and the important role it plays in a student's schooling. This belief is better than any professional development seminar, workshop, training, or conference I have experienced. And while professional development trainings can be very beneficial, the training my staff needed first was not to be found in outside experiences but in learning how to function together and become a PLC. They were in need of job-embedded professional development along with those outside workshops and conferences.

Job-embedded professional learning is

> learning that is grounded in day-to-day practice and is designed to enhance professional practice with the intent of improving children's learning and development. . . . It consists of teams of professionals assessing and finding solutions for authentic and immediate problems of practice as part of a cycle of continuous improvement. (Pacchiano, Klein, & Hawley, 2016, p. 7)

They needed the necessary tools to become a PLC, and they had to make some paradigm shifts to build those tools for themselves. These shifts started with a shared belief, and they leveraged what they already believed to open their minds to new ideas and to learning new things.

PLCs and the Importance of Effective Early Childhood Programs

Implementing the PLC process in early childhood education can increase student learning. In their study of exemplary preschools, psychologist Hirokazu Yoshikawa et al. (2013) "report strong evidence that preschools boost children's language, literacy, and math skills in the short term; it may also reduce problem behaviors such as aggression" (p. 1). Their report states that high-quality preK programs are associated with larger effect sizes; the teachers at these schools have time to collaborate and use the tools of a PLC (Yoshikawa et al., 2013). Yoshikawa et al. (2013) also report that there is evidence of a positive and statistically significant relationship between teacher collaboration and student success.

President George W. Bush created the President's Commission on Excellence in Special Education in October 2001. In July 2002, the commission released its findings and recommendations in *A New Era: Revitalizing Special Education for Children and Their Families* (U.S. Department of Education Office of Special Education and Rehabilitative Services, 2002). One of the highlights of this report was the evidence in its findings indicating the importance of early intervention. In July 2013, Karen E. Diamond, Laura M. Justice, Robert S. Siegler, and Patricia A. Snyder released a research synthesis that supports this conclusion. Their report states that early childhood programs are "particularly important for closing the gap in early skills among children experiencing risk factors relative to more-advantaged children" (Diamond et al., 2013, p. 37).

Early childhood, beginning in infancy, is a period of profound advancement in reasoning and language acquisition for children. The achievement gap between U.S. students of differing income classes and between different races and ethnicities appears even before kindergarten (President's Council of Economic Advisors [PCEA], 2014). Early childhood programs are opportunities to make a dent in closing this gap, but only if their quality is high. This means that early educators have a potentially large role in shaping this gap closure.

Researchers have confirmed that attending a preschool program prior to entering kindergarten has significant positive effects on students. Favorable outcomes in cognition, social skills, and school progress were noted to have the highest results (Smith, 2014). In a National Institute for Early Education Research policy brief, the research confirms that participation in a preschool program improves a student's academic achievement regardless of background or personal circumstances (Barnett, Brown, & Shore, 2004). Early childhood researcher and professor Anne B. Smith (2014) confirms, "High-quality, intensive ECE programs have positive effects on cognitive development, school achievement and completion, especially for low-income children in model programs designed to ameliorate poverty" (p. 3).

Research also reveals that preschools offering high-quality programs and superior teachers can do the following: they narrow the achievement gap for all students, lead to greater education attainment and higher earnings as adults, lower involvement with the criminal justice system, and reduce the need for remedial education and special education placement (Barnett et al., 2004; Meloy, Gardner, & Darling-Hammond, 2019).

The evidence is clear that students with better early childhood care and education grow up to be more likely to work, earn higher wages, have better health, pay more in taxes, and draw on fewer government resources. Author and educator

Jonathon Saphier (2005) asserts that PLCs improve teachers and their teaching. Better teaching, in turn, improves student learning. PLCs provide teachers with the opportunity to improve their teaching and to ensure that all students learn at high levels. They can supply students with programs before they enter the K–12 system that will better their chances of success in their adult lives. The bottom line is that the earlier we intervene, the more effective we will be. The better our early childhood programs are, the more successful our students will be. Through the PLC process, we can make our programs better so that *all* students learn at high levels.

The Challenges of Collaboration for Early Childhood Educators

Due to "organizational differences, it is not a straightforward task to apply elementary practices to early childhood classroom settings" (Diamond et al., 2013, p. 39). Differences in schedules, professional development opportunities, and financial compensation for teachers create a chasm between preK staff and the rest of the elementary school staff. A pattern emerges in which collaborative curriculum planning for general education teachers, special education teachers, and preschool teachers is not very organized. There is often a disconnect between preK teachers and elementary teachers. Collaboration between these teachers is often limited and more separate than coordinated. These groups of teachers tend to plan individually rather than together (Nilsen, 2017).

Being the only preK teacher in a building can be overwhelming. When I taught preschool, my classroom was in a mobile unit outside the school building. Talk about being isolated. This feeling does not have to be the case. Schools and districts that function as PLCs have access to collaborative processes that can support teachers of young children. Policymakers and educators alike often think about early education, special education, and general education as three separate systems. This conception needs to change. PreK programs need to be considered as part of the traditional K–12 school system. Your programs are part of the education continuum.

A cultural shift in all classrooms and settings that serve young children needs to take place to implement the PLC process. PreK teachers need to see themselves as part of the total school. Collaborating across grade levels gives teachers the opportunity for fresh insight and support. For example, maybe a teacher of a higher grade level has novel ideas about how you could build algebraic thinking skills for kindergarteners. Teachers and schools must take collective responsibility for the learning of *all* students and the belief that all students can learn at high levels.

Think about a child who is important to you. Is it a son, daughter, niece, nephew, or grandchild? Why is this child so important? What is it that you wish for his or her future? Of course, you want the best for your loved one, and you would do almost anything in your power for this child to succeed and to learn at the highest levels possible. You would want him or her to go to the best schools and have the best teachers. I probably don't need to do much to convince you that it's imperative to think of every student like he or she is your important child. Every early childhood educator begins to build the foundation of learning and love in their students that will last a lifetime. Don't underestimate your role in students' lifelong school success. At Willow Grove, staff brought photos of their most important child and posted them in the staff lounge under the heading "Is It Good Enough for Them?" as a daily reminder that *all* students are important.

About This Book

The focus of this book is to outline the major concepts of PLCs and to make it clear how educators of young children can apply and use these concepts in early childhood settings in order to fully integrate with the whole-school or whole-district PLC. Many of the ideas and tools may already be in place in your school, but you may not be using them. You may be meeting and discussing issues with your colleagues together as a team, but you may not be focusing on the *right things*—the things that will make a difference in a student's education at its very early stages.

This book provides clarity on the key ideas and concepts that are the building blocks of PLCs. It shares supportive ideas for teachers and staff who work with the youngest learners—those students in kindergarten, early childhood special education programs, preK programs, birth-to-three programs, and Head Start (https://acf.hhs.gov/ohs). It asserts that teachers of young children are critical participants in a school's journey to becoming a PLC, a place that ensures that all students learn at high levels. It also confirms the important place that early childhood programs have in a schoolwide or districtwide PLC.

This book illustrates how to face the challenges of PLC implementation and how to use the tools and processes of a PLC to move forward. My aim is to give direction and meaning to the PLC process for early educators while providing answers to questions about the practice. I share methodologies, approaches, techniques, and procedures useful to early educators adopting and engaging in the PLC process.

The chapters in this book focus on how teachers of children in early childhood programs fit into and function in their school- or districtwide PLC. Chapter 1 discusses the importance of high-quality early childhood programs and what successful schools and programs have done. Chapter 2 illustrates the building blocks of a PLC and how they fit into early childhood programs. I discuss the four critical questions that drive the work of a PLC and the three big ideas that inform them. Chapter 2 also defines the need for a strong mission, an enduring vision, powerful value statements that are mindful of early childhood, and challenging but attainable goals to drive progress. Chapter 3 explains the different types of teams that early childhood educators need to participate in. This chapter sheds light on what these teams do when they meet and the importance of making sure everyone hears the *early childhood voice*. I provide examples of tools that teams can use to streamline their meetings and put their time to good use. Most of these tools were originally designed for traditional K–12 PLCs, and I include them here with no revisions; the principles that guide PLCs are as applicable to early childhood classrooms as they are to upper-level classrooms. Chapter 4 explains the necessary shift in mindset from teaching to learning and goes into how to develop a guaranteed and viable curriculum by identifying essential standards. It addresses the first of the four critical questions: What do we want students to know and be able to do? It includes a protocol that illustrates the steps in a process for determining early childhood essential standards. It also discusses how to pace the curriculum to ensure that all standards are taught and assessed and that students are learning the essential standards. Chapter 5 addresses the second critical question (How do we know they are learning it?) about assessments and what they look like for preK students. It details the importance of appropriate assessments and gives some ideas on how to administer them. Finally, chapter 6 discusses data and what to do with them. This chapter explains how to use data to determine student learning and to better your own teaching skills. It offers a protocol with specific steps for data analysis. Lastly, this chapter looks at the third and fourth critical questions (What do we do when they have not learned it? What do we do when they have already learned it?). I touch on response to intervention (RTI) and what the similarities and differences are between RTI at the early childhood level and in K–12. Also, I focus on how to provide enrichment for those students who have already achieved learning targets.

In your PLC journey, you become committed to the outcome that *all* students learn and achieve at the highest levels. Believe it or not, the practices of a PLC infuse every single aspect of a school's operation. Whether you are new to the PLC process or used to schools that operate as PLCs, you will see that the PLC process makes everything look different than before. Teachers no longer go into their classrooms, close the door, and teach. They focus on student learning, collaboration, and continuous improvement for all stakeholders from the youngest to the oldest, from the gifted to the disabled. The educators who form the PLC share a belief that student learning is the glue that holds the team together.

Chapter 1

The Need for High-Quality Early Childhood Programs

Alone we can do so little, together we can do so much.
—Helen Keller

If you are a teacher of young children, an important question to ask yourself is, "Why did I get into this profession, and why did I become a teacher of young children?" Was it because you wanted a job that would allow you the summers off? Was it because of the great salary? Maybe it was because the hours were shorter and there were a lot of paid days off? You may even love to change diapers and wipe runny noses. I don't think so. Hopefully, most of you got into this profession for the same reason I did, which is because you love seeing that lightbulb come on when students *get it* or when they are so proud of themselves for their accomplishments. You love to see students make breakthroughs and you rejoice in their successes, because as their teacher, you know how hard it was for them to get there. The moments when they realize that they have learned something new about themselves or their world make it all worth it. You delight in engaging students in learning, and you desire to make a difference in their lives.

Each of us could probably share countless stories about the students we have taught. One that stays with me is the day that one of my students took his first steps. At the time he was only able to scoot around on his bottom using his arms to push himself. He was physically disabled with shortened limbs and other obstacles; when he was born, doctors told his parents that he would never walk or do many other things that a typical child does. But this little guy had tenacity. He wanted to move! When he took his first steps, it was as if my own child had started to walk. It was joyful. His parents were over the moon, and the student knew that he had achieved a great accomplishment. Everyone involved was on cloud nine. Another time, I had a teacher in my school whose goal was for one kindergarten student to recognize and count to thirteen. The student would count, "One, two, three, four, five, six, seven, eight, nine, ten, eleven, twelve, *three teen*." We have all been there. You know this student! It took weeks and weeks of hard work, practice, and some fun, but when that student achieved success, we practically had a schoolwide celebration.

Most likely you are passionate about learning yourself and want to instill that passion in your students. Maybe there was a teacher who inspired you, and you want to pass that inspiration along. Teaching very young children can be extremely demanding, but the rewards are great. Seeing that light bulb go off when a student makes a connection. Seeing the smiles on their faces when they know that they have learned something. Seeing learning happen right there in front of you, through a young child's eyes. What I delight in the most is seeing a student experience something for the very first time. Young children are so open to learning new things and honest in their reactions—sometimes even hilarious. You become their advocate and every day you get to see the impact, big or small, that you have on your students. You can instill in each student a love of learning. That is why we teach young children.

Teaching young children requires more input, time, and energy because it demands more individualized instruction geared to where each student is developmentally. If you are reading this book, I know that you, as a teacher of young children, are committed to and passionate about the profession for reasons that are truly connected to student learning. But committed as you are, you can't do everything yourself. You need a strong program behind you.

In this chapter, I discuss how early childhood programs affect student outcomes, including how students with special needs factor into the equation. I also provide some evidence that PLCs have the potential to greatly improve these outcomes.

Outcomes for Students in Early Childhood Programs

High-quality early childhood programs have many benefits and give students a strong start on the path that leads them to college and careers. There is much research that supports high-quality preschool programs as the best route for a student's future success in school. Researchers first studied students in the Perry Preschool Project (https://evidencebasedprograms.org/programs/perry-preschool-project/) and the Abecedarian Project (www.rand.org/well-being

/social-and-behavioral-policy/projects/promising-practices.html) in the early 1960s, continuing the study of these students through adulthood (Schweinhart et al., 2005). These preschool programs were considered to be high-quality with a focus on positive interpersonal interactions between students and teachers, a well-resourced physical environment, and an effective leader that could provide instructional support to teachers (Workman & Ullrich, 2017).

The PCEA (2015) reports that the early childhood education students received in these two programs increased their cognitive and achievement scores by 0.35 standard deviation, meaning that there was a very small span in the range of results; scores all increased about the same, but they did increase. The report concludes that the benefits later in life outweigh the initial cost of these types of programs (PCEA, 2015). A quality preschool program can narrow the achievement gap, which in turn can boost earnings later in life, reduce the need for remedial education services, lessen involvement with the criminal justice system, and improve work-life balance (PCEA, 2015). Children, families, and society all gain when students attend good preschool programs.

Fortunately, more and more public schools are offering preK programs for children in their district due to increased funding in their states (Friedman-Krauss et al., 2018). Many provide early childhood classrooms that consist of typically developing students and students with special needs. For example, I taught a class of fifteen students: five students who were typically developing, five students at risk, and five students with special needs. Other programs in my experience would offer classrooms consisting of fifteen typical students and five students with special needs. In this case, the classroom teacher may or may not be a special education teacher. Some classes may have a regular education teacher who co-teaches with a special education teacher. There are also preK classrooms that consist of students who are developing typically, students at risk, and students with special needs. The staff configuration in these types of classrooms may comprise a regular education teacher, a special education teacher, and possibly special service providers (such as speech-language pathologists, occupational therapists, and so on). Whatever the makeup of the classroom is, the staff in these classrooms provide services for *all* students and they work together as a collaborative team.

Consider the diversity of the students you teach. You may have typically developing students along with students who have special needs in your classroom. You may have a blended class with a mix of students who are typically developing, students at risk, and students with special needs. My classroom, as noted, consisted of five students who were typically developing, five students who were at risk, and five students with special needs. There was also a classroom that consisted of only students with special needs. Some students in your classrooms may be in danger of not succeeding in school. Many may come from unfavorable backgrounds or conditions that reduce their chances of progressing through school. They may be from low socioeconomic backgrounds, speak English as their second language, have speech and language impairments, or be labeled developmentally delayed. Students who speak another language at home and students identified with disabilities, or who are at risk for developing disabilities, can be on a trajectory for short- and long-term school failure (Karoly, Kilburn, & Cannon, 2005; Robbins, Stagman, & Smith, 2012). These may be the students in your classrooms, many of whom are likely to be in district-supported kindergarten programs, publicly supported early childhood programs, and early intervention programs.

The introduction of these students to the public school system begins when they are three, four, or five years old. Some of you may even provide support for children in birth-to-three programs. As teachers of this age group, your role is critical because you are the first teachers these students meet. Your preschool classroom is where these students gain the tools to be prepared not only for future school experiences but for careers and life in our ever-changing world. Falling behind early can be devastating; research reveals the consequences of being ill prepared for school.

- Researchers Jack P. Shonkoff and Deborah A. Phillips (2000) find that young children who are not ready for kindergarten often become teens who are disenchanted with school and are more likely to drop out. These findings are born out again and again (Karoly et al., 2005; Robbins et al., 2012).

- Young children who are not ready for kindergarten tend to carry academic and social-emotional delays with them throughout their education experience (Gormley, Phillips, & Gayer, 2008; Magnuson, Ruhm, & Waldfogel, 2007; Saluja, Scott-Little, & Clifford, 2000; Snow, 2006).

- Problems in school achievement for these students often manifest in higher special education rates, grade repetition, and dropping out of school at twice the rate of their peers (Karoly et al., 2005; Robbins et al., 2012; U.S. Department of Education Office of Special Education and Rehabilitative Services [OSERS], 2002).

- According to the U.S. Department of Justice, "the link between academic failure and delinquency, violence, and crime is welded to reading failure" (as cited in HuffPost, 2017).
- Meanwhile, "85 percent of all juveniles who interface with the juvenile court system are functionally illiterate, and over 70 percent of inmates in America's prisons cannot read above a fourth grade level" (HuffPost, 2017).

Additionally, students of poverty have been over-identified for special education services and remedial support (Isaacs, 2012). Many of these students participate in your district preschool programs. They start elementary school at "a disadvantage in terms of their early skills, behaviors, and health" (Isaacs, 2012, p. 1). Due to lack of preparation for academics, they fall further and further behind and require more services and interventions to support their learning. There were many times as a principal that I felt that if only the students had a little more time and assistance early on, they might not have needed support or services later in their academic careers.

Like programs for other ages, high-quality early childhood programs help *all* students succeed. And the best way to have a high-quality program is to have high-quality teaching. "In the most effective teachers' classrooms, students from disadvantaged backgrounds learn as much as those from advantaged backgrounds. The impact of teacher quality is, indeed, profound" (Solution Tree, 2018, p. 2).

Interestingly, we know how many students qualify for special education services, but do we know how many no longer qualify for services? Do we know how many preschoolers who are at risk go on to the elementary grades requiring no special services? More important, do we know how many preschool students qualify for special education services because they have participated in low-quality preschool programs or didn't attend preschool at all?

The purpose of the Individuals With Disabilities Education Improvement Act (IDEA, 2004) was to give students with special needs access to the general education curriculum in the regular education classroom, but how many students actually exit special education? Is it 20, 10, 5 percent? Special education administrators must compile and submit copious amounts of data on special education students but are not required to report on how many students no longer qualify for services (Friziellie, Schmidt, & Spiller, 2016). In fact, "a very small percentage of those who qualify for special education actually ever get out of the services" (Friziellie et al., 2016, p. 8).

Neuroscientist G. Reid Lyon and colleagues (2001) note federal accountability systems pay little attention to whether students placed in special education at a young age are advancing in core subjects or acquiring the skills necessary for making special education and accommodations no longer necessary. The primary focus of OSERS (2014) was to ensure that states were meeting procedural requirements. But under its "new framework known as Results-Driven Accountability (RDA), the Department will also include educational results and outcomes for students with disabilities in making each state's annual determination under the Individuals with Disabilities Education Act" (OSERS, 2014, p. 1). We are finally turning the corner and realizing that students with disabilities must be held to high standards and can achieve success.

What Successful Teams in Early Childhood Programs Can Accomplish

When a school or district begins the journey of becoming a PLC, it commits to ensuring that *all* students learn at the highest levels. PLCs are popular in the K–12 education system; however, there are only a few early childhood programs actively promoting PLC practices at the preK level (http://allthingsplc.info/evidence). Thus, it is difficult for early childhood educators to find examples of protocols, data, rubrics, and so on that they may use as models for their own programs. At Willow Grove, we had to devise many of our own tools or modify elementary-level models. This may also be the case for your programs. Teachers of young children are generally not using the tools of a PLC, nor are they involved in the PLC process in their schools for the purpose of improving student achievement.

However, the future of PLCs in early childhood programs is limitless. Implementing PLC concepts opens the door for rich, game-changing team discussions about assessments, data, and much more. The team collaboration that grows from the PLC foundation is unendingly valuable. For the PLC process to work for our youngest learners, *all* teachers and staff must be included in and part of the process. The staff at Willow Grove, and the staff of its school district, KCSD 96, embrace the PLC process and live it every day. Our school consists of many different team configurations. There is an early childhood team made up of teachers of young children (three- to five-year-olds). There are early childhood teams whose members include the classroom teacher, speech and language therapist, occupational therapist, physical therapist, social worker, and support staff. Often consultants and coaches participate in teams, too. Kindergarten teachers also

The Need for High-Quality Early Childhood Programs

collaborate in a team that includes the special education teacher who has responsibility for specific students in kindergarten classrooms. All classroom teachers are participants in districtwide vertical teams. The development of these types of teams brings teachers, grade levels, and individual schools together, unifying all members of the district and giving them one purpose: learning for *all* students. I further discuss team configurations in chapter 3 (page 37). As educators of young children, all staff at Willow Grove feel it is their responsibility to ensure that every single student in the school learns at the highest levels.

Willow Grove's success shows that the PLC process can be implemented at all levels of any district or school. Just because you teach young children does not mean that you cannot utilize the tools and premises of your school or district's PLC. Things may look a little different than they do in the elementary grades, but the concepts are the same. The makeup of the teams may vary, and assessments may change. Adaptations may be necessary for early childhood professionals in PLCs due to variations in class size, staffing support, education levels, and so on, but the discussions teachers engage in are the same.

Researchers Vescio, Ross, and Adams (2008) review eight studies that examine the relationship between teacher participation in PLCs and student achievement. They conclude, "The collective results of these studies offer an unequivocal answer to the question about whether the literature supports the assumption that student learning increases when teachers participate in PLCs. The answer is a resounding and encouraging yes" (Vescio et al., 2008, p. 80). To see evidence of the impact of PLCs in action, the first place to look is on the AllThingsPLC website (https://allthingsplc.info). It is full of school success stories.

For example, Julia Goldstein Early Childhood Education Center in University City, Missouri, has seen dramatic increases since 2015 by implementing the PLC process. In its assessments of essential learning objectives in mathematics and literacy, preK student understanding increased throughout each school year by as much as 60 percent (AllThingsPLC, n.d.c).

Another example, Aspen Early Learning Center in Riverton, Wyoming, was created when its school district reconfigured. Staff immediately embraced the PLC process and after three years saw great improvement in both kindergarten and its Kinder Boost program for students not yet ready for kindergarten (figure 1.1, page 16).

Student Achievement Data Fremont County School District No. 25 End-of-Year Kindergarten and Kinder Boost Assessment Data			
Percentage of Students Meeting or Exceeding Proficiency			
Kindergarten			
	2016–2017	2017–2018	2018–2019
Reading Foundational Skills	76 percent		
Reading on Grade Level		76 percent	89 percent
Fluent to 5 in Mathematics	71 percent	74 percent	90 percent
Kinder Boost			
	2016–2017	2017–2018	2018–2019
Reading Foundational Skills	67 percent		
Reading on Grade Level		74 percent	64 percent
Making a Pile of 12 in Mathematics	67 percent	83 percent	93 percent

Source: AllThingsPLC, n.d.b.

FIGURE 1.1: Student learning improvements at Aspen Early Learning Center.

Another success, Alcott Elementary School, in Hastings, Nebraska, also illustrates how the PLC process can help a school weather forces beyond its control. Alcott saw years of improvement in its kindergarten through second-grade students with the PLC process (AllThingsPLC, n.d.a). This school acquired data through the Dynamic Indicators of Basic Early Literacy Skills (DIBELS), a set of procedures and measures for assessing the acquisition of early literacy skills from kindergarten through sixth grade. As you'll see in figure 1.2, literacy scores for kindergarten through second grade were still steadily increasing from 2012 to 2016 before experiencing a decrease.

Alcott Elementary School			
Percentage of students meeting end-of-year benchmark: Alcott score/state score			
Year	DIBELS Kindergarten	DIBELS First Grade	DIBELS Second Grade
2017–2018	84/78	71/67	64/70
2016–2017	88/77	67/69	50/71
2015–2016	91/84	63/75	70/73
2014–2015	89/85	81/74	64/72
2013–2014	89/79	81/65	69/73
2012–2013	84/74	64/65	56/58

Note: Reading tests changed to English language arts with new standards in 2016–2017.
Source: Adapted from AllThingsPLC, n.d.a.

FIGURE 1.2: Alcott Elementary School data 2012–2018.

The school's robust team structures already in place allowed staff to recognize and diagnose the problem, which it attributed to changes in the assessment, a new testing platform, and a physical move from a temporary structure back to the original school building (AllThingsPLC, n.d.a). The teachers have redoubled their efforts and commitment to the PLC process, and scores have begun to rebound. I chose this example to help illustrate how the PLC process is not just something schools do once. It's an ongoing process of continuous improvement.

Widely respected education researcher Robert J. Marzano (2003) concludes that "an analysis of research conducted over a thirty-five-year period demonstrates that the schools that are highly effective produce results that almost entirely overcome the effects of student backgrounds" (p. 7). In my experience, teachers use the lack of outside resources, not enough time in the school day, and poor home and family life as the reasons behind their students' failings. Creating positive change in a school takes a lot of hard work, but it is passion and conversation that spark positive change, and this is necessary. By implementing the practices, procedures, and beliefs of a PLC, you draw forth that passion, you start those conversations, and you begin the difficult, systemic work of change. PLCs don't require extra money or a new curriculum that must be implemented. They don't require an expert to come in and work with staff and students; the most important experts are those who work in the classrooms every day—the teachers. In a PLC, you don't have to work harder, you work smarter.

Author Douglas B. Reeves (2003, 2019) conducted a study in Milwaukee, Wisconsin, which affirms the fact that teachers working together have a profound impact on student achievement. Reeves (2003) researches inner urban schools with 90 percent of their students eligible for free and reduced lunch and 90 percent from ethnic minorities. He collected data over four years and finds that 90 percent of the students meet state or district academic standards in reading and one other area. Factors that led to this success include teachers focusing on academic achievement, making clear curriculum choices, offering frequent assessments with an opportunity for students to improve, emphasizing nonfiction writing, and collaboratively scoring student work (Reeves, 2003, 2019). By focusing on these items, teachers became more effective and provided quality teaching, and students achieved higher levels of learning.

Educator and author Michael Fullan (2008) also studied what successful schools have done and concludes that they focus on student work through assessment, capacity building, collaboration, and the use of ideas and strategies associated with continuous improvement. If you are familiar with PLCs, you might recognize in these the three big ideas of a PLC: (1) a focus on learning, (2) a culture of collaboration, and (3) a focus on results. If not, don't worry—we'll discuss these and other building blocks of a PLC in chapter 2 (page 21).

Early childhood educators often become stuck on the term *assessment*. They find it difficult to appropriately assess their young students and collect data. Many feel that it interferes with their instruction, or that they conduct assessments but do not use the information. Many even feel that assessment of young students just plain doesn't allow for accuracy (Fullan, 2000). To be clear, teachers should use assessment during instruction so they can gather feedback to adjust their teaching to improve students' learning and achievement of targets and standards. I discuss this issue further in chapter 5, where I provide examples to show how you can effectively assess your students and how to use the data to improve your instruction.

Saphier (2005) notes that PLCs produce more good teachers more of the time. In other words, PLCs improve teaching, which improves student results, especially for the least advantaged. Saphier (2005) believes that if schools focus on teacher quality, they will in turn improve their schools. The best way to raise teacher quality is to engage collaborative teams in conversations that promote learning. Teachers of young children need to have these types of conversations with their colleagues. These are different than those discussions that revolve around personal stories and opinions. Teachers of young children in PLCs are committed to asking probing questions and inviting their colleagues to observe and review their teaching and their students' learning. We need to develop the capacity of the teachers in our schools, because a school is only as good as the people in it. By improving teachers, we can improve the quality of instruction. Effective teachers have an impact on student achievement, and ineffective teachers can impede the learning of their students. There is research to support that teacher quality has a lasting effect on student performance with a larger impact on learning (Friedman, 2018). Unfortunately, the opposite is true, and one year with an ineffective teacher may cause students to take years to catch up with peers (Friedman, 2018).

Outcomes like the ones I've described in this chapter sound great. But what do schools do to achieve such dramatic results with their students, especially their youngest learners? How are they making student success a reality? How are these schools closing the gap? Being part of a PLC will help you grow your own practice in order to be as effective as you can be. Beginning in the following chapter, I discuss exactly how to make this success a reality. I start by explaining some PLC basics to help you get started.

Chapter 2

The Building Blocks of a PLC

There is no power for change greater than a community discovering what it cares about.

—Margaret Wheatley

The PLC process is not just a possibility for early childhood programs; rather, it is an *essential* pathway to success. Before you can begin the PLC journey, however, it's important to understand what a PLC is. This chapter focuses on the basic principles, the foundation, of a PLC. PLCs center on student learning through the work of collaborative teams. These teams build shared knowledge using action research. Mission, vision, values, and goals are all integral elements of a PLC's foundation. These are all important pieces for early childhood educators to understand and put into practice.

However, first, let's be clear about what a PLC is not. A PLC is not a meeting that you go to on Tuesday, or a book study, or a new initiative (that will be replaced next year by something else). If the preschool teachers say, "We had our PLC meeting," then you know there is not a clear understanding of what a PLC represents. Collaboration may focus on the nuts and bolts of school culture; a large number of attendees in one single meeting makes this collaboration unwieldy. In contrast, teachers at Willow Grove have many meetings for many different purposes, but the bottom line is that all the meetings focus on student learning. It is one thing to say that you are a PLC and quite another to create a culture where the PLC can thrive. The PLC process is *about how a school functions every day*. PLC experts Richard DuFour, Rebecca DuFour, Robert Eaker, Thomas W. Many, and Mike Mattos (2016) define a PLC as:

> An ongoing process in which educators work collaboratively in recurring cycles of collective inquiry and action research to achieve better results

> for the students they serve. PLCs operate under the assumption that the key to improved learning for students is continuous job-embedded learning for educators. (p. 10)

The PLC process is "a continuous, never-ending process of conducting schooling that has a profound impact on the structure and culture of the school and the assumptions and practices of the professionals within it" (DuFour et al., 2016, p. 10). It is the collaborative process that teachers at any level, including teachers of young children, can benefit from. It is a team of people sharing and critically interrogating their practice in an ongoing, reflective, collaborative, inclusive, learning-oriented, and growth-promoting way (Mitchell & Sackney, 2000; Toole & Louis, 2002). The educators in a school or district who form a PLC share the belief that student learning is at the core of their mission. Shouldn't student learning be the basis of a school's mission regardless of the age of the student?

The PLC process contains central ideas, or building blocks, that work in concert to support student learning. These include the three big ideas, the four critical questions, and the four pillars.

The Three Big Ideas of a PLC

The relentless focus on student learning is the first of three big ideas that form the core of PLCs (DuFour et al., 2016).

1. Focus on learning
2. Culture of collaboration
3. Focus on results

These principles guide every aspect of a PLC. Professor and school improvement expert Karen Seashore Louis (2006) reiterates that the critical role of a PLC is the persistent effort of teachers to "focus on the relationship between their practice and the bottom line—student learning" (p. 479). In other words, "strong PLCs have teachers working together more effectively as they put more effort into creating and sustaining opportunities for student learning" (Kruse, Louis, & Bryk, 1994, p. 4).

And it's not just student learning; teachers in a PLC are constantly learning as well. Teachers learn from one another and create opportunities for themselves to express and to share qualities (Caruso, 2007). Who better to learn from than other early childhood teachers? An added value is that much teacher growth can stem from learning from one another through collaboration. By learning this way, good teachers become better, and better teachers become the best. Yes, there will be lengthy team conversations at every level, but they will be purposeful conversations about student learning and how all teachers can help students achieve success. Early childhood teachers can learn from one another in their meetings, and they can apply this learning in their own classrooms. Many teachers report that, through these discussions, they better understand some principles of education and they fuse what they discuss into the curriculum they are implementing in their classrooms. You can think of your team as an amazing resource that's right there to use: "In a PLC, each teacher within a collaborative team has access to the ideas, materials, strategies, and talents of the entire team" (Honawar, 2008, p. 26).

PLCs require a culture of mutual accountability. That mutual accountability includes all stakeholders, beginning with the teachers of young children. Teachers then work collaboratively in pursuit of education goals for their students. PLCs promote a collegial culture and provide capacity building that sustains relationships and open dialogue (Lieberman, 1995; Noguera & Noguera, 2018). Schools that have engaged in the PLC process offer support and motivation to teachers as they work to overcome lack of resources, isolation, time constraints, and other obstacles that schools commonly encounter.

PLCs will bring about change in your school and in your programs. Change can be hard, but the difficulty is part of a process. As I say previously, my school began the process in the early 2000s and is still improving, learning, and growing to this day. PLCs are not formed overnight, and schools must stick with their core principles to sustain success over time. It is a process of continuous improvement (DuFour, 2004; Louis, 2006; Lumpe, 2007; Scribner, 1999; Westheimer, 1999; Wood, 2007). Any school or team that is beginning this change must realize that a long-term commitment is essential (DuFour, 1991). PLCs are about changing the culture within a school; it is not an easy task to alter long-held understandings, beliefs, expectations, and habits. It may be challenging to get some middle school or even elementary school teachers to understand that preschoolers don't just take naps and play all day. Invite them into your classrooms! Let them see your students at work. Help them understand that the work that you are doing now with these students will help them become better learners at the upper grades. Preschool is the beginning of students' academic journey, and where they develop social, emotional, and physical skills. They become familiar with structure, routine, and instruction. They build responsibility, self-sufficiency, and self-confidence. The early education these young students receive is crucial to their future success: "Early childhood education is inextricably linked with broader goals of college and career readiness, largely because early learning builds the foundation for later success" (Guilfoyle, 2013, p. 1). The principal of the middle school in my district always took the time and effort to thank the preschool teachers for preparing students for middle school.

The work is never done. At Willow Grove, we started with baby steps, and as we learned more, we did better and took bigger steps. As I establish in chapter 1, the research-based PLC process increases teacher collaboration, morale, and, more importantly, student learning and achievement in the classroom (Reeves, 2003, 2019; Saphier, 2005). And it takes time. Aspen Early Learning Center can attest to hard work that has paid off; see the evidence on the AllThingsPLC (n.d.b) website. It has seen rising results from 2016 to 2019 in the areas of mathematics and literacy. The focus on results has allowed Aspen to monitor student progress, create a system of interventions, and build effective collaborative teams.

PLCs represent an opportunity for teachers to engage in shared learning and collective discussions that lead to improved student outcomes. In a PLC, things keep improving because educators always look at the results together and use them to achieve new learning and development. The focus of a PLC is the commitment to high levels of learning for every student, no matter the students' ages or the program they are in. Those are the students in your programs and in programs that begin even before a child is three. All teachers must take on a sense of responsibility for the learning of all students in a school or district (Elmore, 2004). It is not just about *your* set of students, but those of the *entire* school or district that should be of concern to all teachers. It is amazing to be a part of and see the growth of a student between the ages of three and five, and everyone in the school can feel it. Everything involved in a PLC flows from embracing the idea of all students learning at high levels, including kindergarteners and preschool students.

The Four Critical Questions of a PLC

In a PLC, collaborative teams understand what it is they're doing and what they need to discuss when they work together. They do this by focusing on four critical questions (DuFour et al., 2016).

1. What do we want students to know and be able to do?
2. How will we know if they have learned it?
3. What will we do if they have not learned it?
4. What will we do if they already know it?

These four questions are a constant guiding force that focuses the work of a PLC no matter what grade level is involved. However, what young students know and can do may not be as cut and dry as in the elementary grades, whose teachers can turn to their defined standards to answer this question. Many states have early childhood standards, but they are inconsistent across the United States. Often schools, teams, or districts must develop these essential standards on their own. At Willow Grove, we looked at the Common Core State Standards (CCSS) for kindergarten (National Governors Association Center for Best Practices [NGA] & Council of Chief State School Officers [CCSSO], 2010a, 2010b) and the Illinois Early Learning and Development Standards for Preschool (Illinois State Board of Education, 2013) to make sure we implemented appropriate learning progressions for students from birth to age five. We used the Illinois standards and the Creative Curriculum objectives (Teaching Strategies, n.d.) to prioritize objectives for our early learners. I will go into further detail about how early childhood educators can develop, vertically align, and use standards in chapter 4 (page 69).

The second critical question addresses assessment. There is a big difference in the way that students are assessed in preschool than in the elementary grades. We do not assess young children with pencil-and-paper or standardized tests. I discuss this further in chapter 5 (page 87).

This difference, not surprisingly, persists as well when taking on the third and fourth questions, which help teams tackle interventions for students who struggle and extensions for students who have achieved proficiency. I cover these topics in greater detail in chapter 6 (page 103), but for now it is important to understand a PLC's essential characteristics, including collective inquiry, action research, and the four pillars: shared mission, vision, values, and goals, and what they might look like in an early childhood setting.

Collective Inquiry

Collaborative teams in a PLC engage in *collective inquiry*, the process of building shared knowledge by clarifying questions that they explore together (DuFour et al., 2016). They investigate their own education practices. They discuss how they teach skills. Every teacher has the professional responsibility to be part of a PLC and engage in collective inquiry. It is not just for the elementary and secondary teachers. Reeves (2010) notes that the collective inquiry process has a measurable and significant effect on student achievement.

To illustrate, I recall a team meeting at Willow Grove in which we noticed that students in Mrs. A.'s kindergarten class were proficient in sight-word recognition by the end of the school year. We assessed this skill throughout the school year with a *common assessment*—that is, one that the teachers designed as a team and administered to all classes. When we asked her how she accomplished this, she just stated that she worked really hard with her students. No! How did she specifically teach this skill? What strategies did she utilize? She finally revealed one of her strategies: each time her students left the classroom for recess, home, gym class, and so on, they had to name the sight word that she held on a card at the door. It's an easy strategy that some teachers never thought of. Now they could use it themselves to the benefit of all.

After the experience with Mrs. A., we decided to have specific collaborative team meetings that we called *shop and share*. Each teacher would bring an example to team meetings of how he or she taught a specific target and demonstrate it. For example, at one preK meeting we discussed a standard we had adopted from the Illinois Early Learning and Development Standards: "Recognize, duplicate, extend, and create simple patterns in various formats" (8.A.ECb; Illinois State Board of Education, 2013). Teachers shared examples of how their students would make patterns with toy vehicles (by color or type), with their body movement (jump, step, jump, step), or even with instruments (bang, tap, bang, tap). Some teachers even brought video clips of their classes producing these patterns.

Engaging in collective inquiry is the way that teachers approach decision making as they gather evidence. Teacher teams ask questions about the learning of their young students. They develop theories, establish action plans, and take the necessary steps to improve their teaching and student learning. They gather evidence to assess the impact of their actions. If we had never collected data on sight words, we never would have known that Mrs. A. was getting the best results, and we never would have learned what she did to get them. Even at the preK level, we were able to notice individual teachers who had students with higher proficiencies on specific skills. Subsequently, teams begin to think differently, and many long-standing beliefs change. Teachers begin to learn that their way may not always be the best way, and if it is, they should share it for the benefit of all students. High-performing school systems use collective inquiry to create and sustain a strong profession (Patankar, 2013).

These schools exemplify enthusiasm to question, experiment, and design new teaching methods. Educators participating in collective inquiry examine *external evidence* (such as research) and *internal evidence* (which teachers are getting the best results) together as a team. They explore best practices in teaching and in student learning. By doing this, teachers can make well-informed decisions about their own teaching practices and determine whether their students are learning.

Teachers can develop new skills and capabilities from their peers and from current research and data to enhance their teaching practices. Much growth comes from learning from one another and teacher collaboration: "In a professional learning community, each teacher has access to the ideas, materials, strategies, and talents of the entire team of teachers" (Honawar, 2008, p. 26). Teachers can discuss trends in knowledge and expertise of teaching as well as take time to observe peers in the classroom. At Willow Grove, I would often offer to take over a teacher's class so he or she could spend time in a colleague's classroom. This type of collaboration helps develop teaching that enhances student learning. It is not about who is the best teacher; it is about using all teachers' individual strengths to benefit all.

Action Research

Through *action research* teachers work together to become more proficient at identifying and solving problems (AllThingsPLC, 2016). They turn research into aspiration and move quickly to turn aspiration and visions into action and action into reality. They evaluate, investigate, and analyze research to learn and improve programs and education techniques. They "understand that the most powerful learning always occurs in the context of taking action, and they value engagement and experience as the most effective teachers" (DuFour, DuFour, Eaker, & Many, 2010, p. 12). Teachers try "new practices and procedures and then measure their impact on student learning to determine if the change was beneficial" (Mattos, DuFour, DuFour, Eaker, & Many, 2016, p. 6). They believe in experimentation. Just because the school has always done something a certain way does not necessarily make it right. As a principal, I used to separate twins when they entered kindergarten. At some point, a mother of twins asked me why I did this, and my response was, "I've always done it this way." The mother offered me an abundance of articles and research on the drawbacks of separating twins at the early childhood level. I shared this information with staff, and our newfound knowledge moved us to make changes to what we had always done. We used action research to gain knowledge and to make an informed decision.

The process of action research consists of four steps (Jakicic, 2019).

1. Formulating the problem
2. Identifying and implementing a strategy to address the problem
3. Creating a process for gathering evidence of the effectiveness of the strategy
4. Collecting and analyzing the evidence to then make decisions based on that evidence

We brought the problem of twin placement to the kindergarten team: Should twins be placed in separate or the same classrooms when entering kindergarten? Teachers wanted to better understand the reason or reasons to separate or not to separate twins in class. They determined that each teacher would individually collect current research on the issue. At their next team meeting they would then share the highlights of their research. After sharing and discussing the research they brainstormed a list of pros and cons. They noted that placement of twins together could actually be better for the students, and we resolved that it should be the parents' decision whether to separate their twins or not. The research, discussion, and agreement of a group of teachers led to a positive change.

The Four Pillars of a PLC

The foundation of a PLC "rests on the four pillars of mission, vision, values, and goals" (DuFour et al., 2010, p. 30). Every school or district has its own unique mission, vision, values, and goals that form its pillars. The pillars codify a set of guiding principles that articulate what the people in the school believe and what they collectively commit to do. These guiding principles are embedded in the hearts and minds of the people in the school from the custodian to the administrator. I specifically mention custodian because ours was very involved. At dismissal time when the students were lined up to go home, he would throw the ball to each student in line and play catch. He was embodying the school's values and vision by working on gross motor skills. There must be a shared mission, vision, values, and goals that all members of the school community agree with and feel passionate about. Figure 2.1 illustrates the underlying principles of a PLC and how each pillar asks a different question. Early childhood educators can just as easily answer these questions as a K–12 teacher. They can simply team up with teachers at higher grade levels and join their conversations around a school's mission, vision, values, and goals. When educators have answered these questions, they have then established a solid foundation for their PLC. The following sections discuss each pillar in more detail.

Mission

Mission statements give school staff something in writing that clearly states their school's views. They act as a guide when working in a team and can be quite valuable when you get lost in details that blur your vision, such as bus schedules, parent involvement, supply lists, and so on. Many times, teams need to stop and reflect on the school's mission before they move forward. At Willow Grove, there were times when we stopped our discussions and asked, "Is this what is best for the students, or is this what is best (easiest) for the teachers?" The mission of a

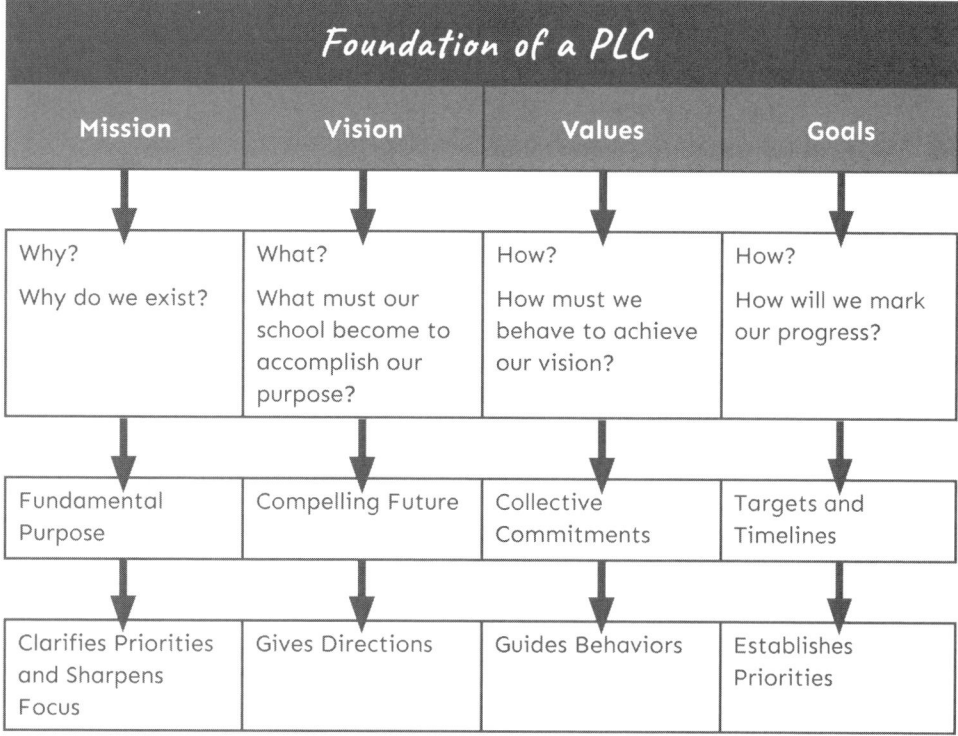

FIGURE 2.1: The four pillars of a PLC.

school or district is not something that a group of people or a committee or an administrative team writes; it is something they live. Just writing a mission statement does nothing to change how people act (Pfeffer & Sutton, 2000). It must be a collaborative effort by actual teachers, along with administrators, and it takes time. Dialogue engages people and attaches meaning to their work. In a school or district with a large staff, a guiding coalition may write the mission, vision, values, and goals. The *guiding coalition,* "an alliance of key members of an organization who are specifically charged with leading a change process" (Mattos et al., 2016, p. 21), should include current staff members and cover all disciplines. That means that educators of young children should be represented and be actively engaged in the discussion, even if it means insisting on a seat at the table. Early childhood staff play an important role and should not be left out.

Once the guiding coalition members have created a draft, they share it with all stakeholders, including early childhood educators, all teachers and support staff, and the community in order to solicit input and feedback. These conversations and discussions that take place when developing a mission statement trigger further action. Teachers view it as a pledge. Truthful conversations are an important step in forming collaborative teams. The mission of Hastings Public Schools in Hastings, Nebraska, is: "Our fundamental purpose is to [ensure] all students acquire the knowledge, skills, and behaviors essential to be successful individuals and responsible citizens" (Hastings Public Schools, n.d.).

You can look up a hundred mission statements online that were developed by schools, districts, and businesses—they can offer inspiration, but they are not really yours. They have no real meaning for you, your school, your programs, or your students. The reflective dialogue that takes place when a school or district comes together to write a mission statement is invaluable. It is why preschool teachers should discuss the draft mission statement for their school to make sure and be clear that it captures their views and reflects the mission of their programs. This is an opportunity for all staff members to understand and hear how important the services that the teachers of young children provide are to the mission of the school. This is the time for all to be heard. A mission statement is the culmination of vision, values, and goals. Your school's mission statement should explain why you exist. Mission statements separate what is important and what is not. They identify what the school is going to accomplish.

The mission statement should focus on learning, as this is what guides decisions and establishes the priorities for *all* students:

> School mission statements that promise "learning for all" have become a cliché. But when a school staff takes that statement literally—when teachers view it as a pledge to ensure the success of each student rather than a politically correct hyperbole—profound changes begin to take place. (DuFour, 2004, p. 10)

For example, School District 54 in Schaumburg, Illinois, has the following mission statement: "The mission of School District 54 is to Ensure Student Success. We know that mission is only achieved through the cooperative work of students and staff, and the support of the students' parents and the community at large" (Schaumburg School District 54, n.d.). Your school's mission statement is applicable to all the students in your school, including young children and those with disabilities. Students who have severe disabilities may have difficulties and find it nearly impossible to reach the standards for their grade level. These students need to achieve their own personal maximum potential, and the school's mission statement should encompass them as well.

Figure 2.2 is a protocol that you can use when your school or team is developing a mission statement. This protocol outlines a shared collaborative process that is all-inclusive and engages all members of the team.

Creating a Learning Mission

Recall the two fundamental assumptions undergirding a school's mission to provide high levels of learning for all students: (1) Educators believe that all students are capable of high levels of learning, and (2) they assume the responsibility to make this outcome a reality for every child. This exercise offers a process to create a common mission of learning.

Step 1: Create Individual Mission Statements

Have staff members sit in teams. Ask each person to write a response in eight to twelve words to the question, "What is the fundamental purpose (mission) of our school? In other words, why does our school exist?"

Step 2: Share Individual Mission Statements

Ask each person to share his or her answer and ask a team member to chart the responses. Once all team members have shared, have each team discuss how the responses are similar and how they are different. Then inquire, "How can we work collaboratively to help our students if we have different missions for our school?"

Step 3: Create Team Mission Statements

Have each team create a collective mission statement in eight to twelve words. The purpose is not to combine all the ideas into a comprehensive "laundry list," but rather to find consensus on your school's single most important purpose.

Step 4: Share Team Mission Statements

Ask each team to share its mission statement with the entire group and chart the answers. Ask, "How are our responses similar? How are they different?"

Step 5: Create a School Mission Statement

Using the team statements as a resource, create a collective mission statement of eight to twelve words for your school. Again, reach consensus on the single most important purpose of your school and do not combine all the ideas or make a laundry list.

Step 6: Check Alignment

In a PLC, the fundamental purpose of a school must be learning. It is not a school's mission to ensure that all students are taught, but rather that all students learn. To this end, ask, "Does our final school mission embrace learning?"

Source: Adapted from Buffum, Mattos, & Weber, 2009.

FIGURE 2.2: Protocol for developing a mission statement.

*Visit **go.SolutionTree.com/PLCbooks** for a free reproducible version of this figure.*

Vision

The vision of a school or district is revealed by answering the questions, What do we hope to become at some point in the future? What does our school need to move forward? What do our programs need to move forward? Every school needs a vision that all staff recognize as a common direction of growth, something that inspires them to be better. An effective vision announces to parents and students where you are heading and why you are going there. It connects teachers at every grade level and helps them begin to think deeply about teaching. A school's vision should inspire, motivate, and engage people in moving forward.

Once again, the guiding coalition takes the lead in developing a school's vision statement. Remember that all stakeholders need to be represented on this team. School administrators can make this happen, and early childhood teachers can advocate for themselves to be included. All early childhood educators have thoughts on their school's vision. The guiding coalition assesses the current reality of the school and potential programs, processes, and strategies that need improvement to achieve the vision. Members of the guiding coalition bring their findings to the staff in small group settings to "solicit feedback, clarify ideas, make revisions, and ultimately build consensus on the statement until it represents the shared vision of the members of the organization" (Mattos et al., 2016, p. 23). Teachers of young children should receive the opportunity to think about and discuss the vision they have for their students, programs, and school. This means time (team meeting time, professional development days) and a venue in which these discussions can occur.

The vision is an important part of creating the structures and culture that ensure *all* students learn, right down to the youngest learners. It is applicable to all students in the school from the youngest to the oldest and used as a blueprint for improvement by establishing direction and identifying the compelling future of the school and all its programs. In order to achieve the mission, educators create this common vision of the school they hold as ideal for their students. The Adel DeSoto Minburn Community School District (n.d.) in Adel, Iowa, provides an example of focusing on how current practice can achieve future ideals: "Experiencing Success Today, Achieving Dreams Tomorrow." All teachers want their students to enjoy thriving, productive lives in a future they create.

Values

The values of an organization are the collective commitments that guide the conduct of the group members as educators. They not only guide but "clearly describe how each person can contribute to the improvement initiative" (DuFour, 2015, p. 110). They are the attitudes and behaviors that each person on staff exhibits. Every single person in the school should adopt these behaviors. *Every single person* includes all grade-level staff, all support staff, and all administrators. DuFour (2015) compares the values of a school to the collective commitments that teachers uphold in their classrooms. At the beginning of the school year, many preschool teachers sit down with their students and discuss how they will all act in the classroom (see figure 2.3 for an example of what preschool classroom rules might look like). They answer questions like, Will we be kind? Will we share? Will we speak with an indoor voice? You can harness this same process to make collective commitments for your school.

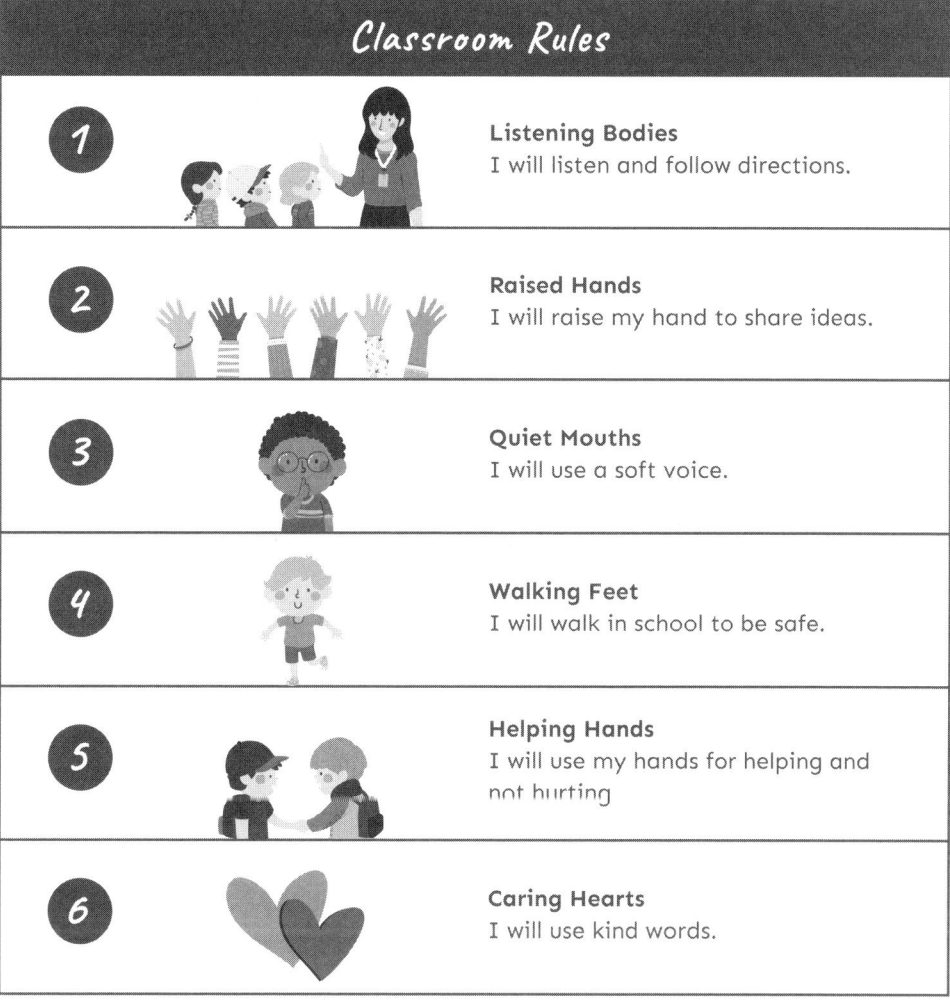

FIGURE 2.3: Rules for a preschool classroom.

Visit *go.SolutionTree.com/PLCbooks* for a free reproducible version of this figure.

Teachers clearly define, teach, and reinforce values with students (DuFour, 2015). School staff must do the same for one another within the daily practice of their PLC. This is how a school goes from a belief to a behavior, from thinking to doing, from *we believe* to *we will*. The key word is *we*. There may be agreement on the mission and vision, but unless there is consensus on what the behavior will look like, then success may be out of reach. Once again, a guiding coalition can write collective commitments and then share them for feedback, but ultimately, once consensus is reached, these commitments guide the behavior of the adults at the school. The following collective commitments guide the behavior of the adults at Kildeer Countryside Community Consolidated School District 96 (KCSD 96, n.d.) in Buffalo Grove, Illinois; they offer an example of what these commitments can look like:

> Model for others what we expect from others—Collective Commitments
> Every child, every school, every day—Collective Commitments
> Best practice, not first practice—Collective Commitments
> Learning has no boundaries—Collective Commitments
> Celebrate success—Collective Commitments

Goals

Districts' goals identify the results they are seeking and provide a way to measure the progress they are making toward those goals. For example, a school district might set a district goal stating that all students are reading at or above grade level by the end of third grade. As a district goal, this is a specific goal, which is ideal. An elementary school in that district would then set a building goal to improve its third graders' reading. If 78 percent of the school's third graders had read at grade level the previous year, it would set a building goal stating that by the end of the school year, 82 percent or more of third graders will be reading at grade level as evidenced by the end-of-year screening tool. This is a realistic goal that directly aligns with the broad district goal of all third-grade students reading at grade level.

Each team's goal (or grade-level goal) should in turn be aligned to the school goals. A second-grade goal could be that 80 percent of students in second grade are reading at grade level (based on last year's data). The end-of-year screener the team is using, for instance, offers a way to ascertain progress toward the goal. Early childhood teams in this district can also develop goals for their students that relate to schoolwide goals. After all, their students too are part of the school. Aligning to the district's goal of third graders reading at grade level, the early childhood teams could focus their goals on prereading skills such as letter recognition, oral language skills, and concepts of print, all of which are necessary to ultimately read at grade level by the end of third grade. For example, a goal for students in early education classes might be this: *By May, 80 percent or more of preschool students eligible for kindergarten will recognize all the letters of the alphabet.*

These goals all have something in common: they are SMART. *SMART goals* are specific, measurable, attainable, results oriented, and time bound (Conzemius

& O'Neill, 2014). Teams in elementary schools can write a SMART goal at the beginning of the school year. These SMART goals (usually one in literacy and one in mathematics) should align with a school's goal of improving literacy and mathematics through cooperative learning strategies, and this in turn would be aligned with the district improvement goal of increasing college and career readiness.

Goals establish the milestones you need to meet in order to achieve the end goal. They are similar to IEP short-term objectives and benchmarks. Goals help sustain momentum toward the mission and provide a pathway to achieve success. Goals also allow for celebrations of small successes. When teams get together to write goals, they practice collective accountability for achieving results. Everyone works toward success.

How the Pillars Work Together

Schools must address each of the four pillars—mission, vision, values, and goals—for a change initiative to have the best chance of success. Addressing the four pillars constitutes initial steps in laying a foundation for making strategic and tactical decisions that will move a school and all its programs forward. Having them in place won't eliminate arguments and disagreements, but disagreement can foster productive discussions if these disagreements happen within the framework the four pillars provide. The pillars can ensure a focused effort to discover how to best get to a mutually agreed-on endpoint as opposed to fruitless tire-spinning in opposite directions. All stakeholders must be involved in the development of their school's mission, vision, values, and goals. As an example, staff members at Boones Mill Elementary School collaborated to create the mission, vision, values, and goals shown in figure 2.4 (page 36). Educators in early childhood or preschool programs can easily apply the same principles.

Mission, vision, value, and goal statements should be accessible to all stakeholders. They were posted in every classroom and in every office at Willow Grove, helping to ingrain them in our hearts and minds.

The four pillars of a PLC, the four critical questions, and the three big ideas all drive the improvement efforts of teachers who have a desire to build a winning education system for their students. They are the foundation and basis for the tireless work that takes place when schools commit to improvement. All this translates into hard work, but it is a powerful way for teachers to work together that will profoundly affect their ways of schooling. In the next chapter, I address how teachers can come together as teams to accomplish this work.

Boones Mill Elementary School: Hand in Hand We All Learn

Mission

It is the mission of Boones Mill Elementary School to ensure high levels of learning for each student. Through mutual respect within the total school community, our children will grow and learn in a positive atmosphere where faculty, staff, students, and parents together are enthusiastic about the teaching and learning process.

Vision

We believe that the most promising strategy for achieving the mission of our school is to develop our capacity to function as a professional learning community. We envision a school in which staff:

- Unite to achieve a common purpose and SMART goals
- Work together—interdependently—in collaborative teams
- Seek and implement promising strategies for improving student learning on a continuous basis
- Monitor each student's progress on a frequent basis
- Demonstrate a personal commitment to the academic success and general well-being of each student

Values

In order to achieve the shared vision of our school, Boones Mill staff have made the following values or collective commitments.

1. Study, clarify, align, and pace state resource guides, assessment blueprints, and district curriculum guides.
2. Develop and implement local common formative assessments to monitor each student's learning.
3. Develop, implement, and evaluate team professional enhancement plans aligned to our SMART goals to target specific instructional areas in need of improvement.
4. Engage in meaningful, job-embedded staff development to enhance our professional skills.
5. Utilize a variety of instructional strategies to promote success for all students.
6. Initiate individual and small-group instructional programs to provide additional learning time for all students.
7. Provide parents with resources, strategies, and information to help students succeed.

Schoolwide Goals

1. To improve student achievement in language arts in each grade level as measured by performance on local, district, state, and national assessments
2. To improve student achievement in math in each grade level as measured by performance on local, district, state, and national assessments

Source: Adapted from DuFour et al., 2016.

FIGURE 2.4: Boones Mill Elementary School mission, vision, values, and goals.

Visit **go.SolutionTree.com/PLCbooks** *for a free reproducible version of this figure.*

Chapter 3

Collaborative Teams in Early Childhood Programs

Teamwork is the ability to work together toward a common vision, the ability to direct individual accomplishments toward organizational objectives. It is the fuel that allows common people to attain uncommon results.

—Andrew Carnegie

This chapter focuses on collaborative teams, how they can make the time to meet, choose the right things to focus on, and provide and respect the roles a variety of teams have in a PLC. It illustrates how teachers of young children can be contributors on many different teams and the importance of their participation. I also offer several tools that teams can use to further their work.

In PLCs, there is a foundational understanding of *how* school staff work together as collaborative teams. Representation by multiple stakeholders in collaborative teams can provide unique and balanced perspectives to fully and accurately analyze data, dig deeper, create hypotheses, and develop solutions. The practices of a PLC not only include regular education teachers and early childhood teachers but must include special educators in the planning and delivery of standards-aligned curriculum, instruction, and assessment. Schools need to consider how all teams fit within the collaborative structure as part of supporting the full range of learners they serve. Early childhood educators bring a special talent to PLCs. Research reveals that special education and preschool teachers' classroom practices, like those of their general education counterparts, often change in a positive direction as a result of their participation in PLCs (Blanton & Perez, 2011). For many schools, especially those with young children or large numbers of pupils with special needs, the role of the early childhood staff can be an important and a critical piece in the PLC process (Louis & Gordon, 2006). You have strategies and resources for teaching basic skills that primary teachers often need. Share your stuff!

Types of Teams

There are many types of collaborative teams that serve essential roles in a healthy PLC. These include grade-level teams, vertical teams, curriculum teams, leadership teams, and problem-solving teams. The following sections provide information about these teams and about how early childhood educators might fit into the teams.

Grade-Level Teams

Teachers at the same grade level can easily form relevant teams and spend time collaborating. If there is more than one early childhood classroom in a building, then these teachers can form a collaborative team and work together for the success of their students. Even if there are only two preK classroom teachers on a team, they can do great work together. I have seen schools that have one preschool classroom for three-year-olds and another classroom for four-year-olds. These teachers can form a team and work on the essential standards for both age groups. Some schools mix the ages in a class and blend these students with those who have special needs or are at risk. These teams can also work on the essential standards for preK students. The question for grade-level teams of early childhood educators is, What do we want our students to know and be able to do to be ready for kindergarten? Any configuration of early childhood teachers can make up a team. After all, they are all working on early childhood skills. The important element is that *every* staff member belongs to a team. These teams connect teachers to their colleagues, and teachers feel supported by them.

The number of teachers on a team can vary, but "the size of the team certainly impacts the way it operates" (Mattos et al., 2016, p. 39). Larger teams may want to subdivide themselves and their responsibilities, and report back later to the larger team. For example, Willow Grove has twelve kindergarten classrooms divided into three teams. Each team has a leader with specific responsibilities. Many times, the principal selects the team leader based on the respect of his or her peers or on leadership potential. The team leader is responsible for organizing and helping the team move forward. The team leader is not a pseudo administrator and does not shoulder the responsibilities of the whole team, address peers or colleagues who choose not to cooperate, or evaluate colleagues' performance. Rather, the leader acts as the liaison between the team and the administration.

His or her responsibilities include planning and distributing the team meeting agenda, facilitating the meeting process, and meeting with other team leaders and administrators. Since the teams also include staff members such as social workers, special education teachers, and so on, the team leader must make sure to provide a team environment that includes and engages the abilities of all its members. At my school, we had one physical education teacher, and she joined a kindergarten team as well as participating on a district-level physical education team. It was important for her to know what skills her kindergarten students were focusing on so that she could incorporate those standards into her physical education lessons. If the weekly target was counting from one to ten, then she would have students in her class take ten steps and count out loud during their warm-up activity.

Sometimes early childhood educators must get creative when forming grade-level teams. Another team configuration could be an early childhood team consisting of preK teachers, Head Start teachers, and early childhood special education teachers. Although these programs may run different curricula, they should have a set of common and aligned expectations for their students. The standards and targets for three-year-olds, no matter what program they are enrolled in, should be the same. Team meetings focus on these expectations. This type of team works on the same outcomes as grade-level teams. They are a grade-level team! The targets and standards should be consistent across programs for each age level. Teachers come together to support one another, learn from one another, and identify ways that they can better meet the needs of their young students.

Many elementary schools have only one kindergarten classroom or one preschool classroom in a building. They may even have only one special education teacher for all students who need services across multiple classrooms. While diversity on teams is important, if like classrooms are scattered across a school district, then schools should take measures to ensure that like team members have time to meet on a weekly basis. This could mean rearranging schedules or changing meeting places. They could all meet at one school or other central location for a staff meeting. They could stay in their building but use their computers to have a virtual meeting. You really may need to think outside the box to accomplish this, but it is a vital component of PLCs. If you are the only teacher who has a preschool class in your building, it is vital to have other preschool teachers to collaborate with. You can still collaborate even if you don't have any obvious team members in your own school: "Educators seeking teammates beyond their school campuses can turn to their district office, regional service center, or professional organizations to find job-alike partners" (DuFour & DuFour, 2012, p. 16). As a teacher, your peers are your most valuable asset, no matter their location or what school district they are in. Meaningful teams may have members who are spread across a district or even across neighboring school districts. The one thing they all need is time to collaborate. They can do this by getting together at a common location or even rotating school sites. What fun it is to visit another teacher's classroom; remember, we are no longer islands unto ourselves.

Vertical Teams

Another opportunity for collaboration is to form vertical teams. Teachers need to know what skills their students learned the previous year and what skills they will need for subsequent years. Vertical teams ensure that students receive a step-by-step, year-by-year curriculum. A vertical team could be a building primary team, which might consist of the kindergarten, first-, and second-grade teachers or the preK, kindergarten, and first-grade teachers, for example. These types of teams link "teachers . . . with those who teach the same content above or below their grade level" (DuFour & DuFour, 2012, p. 16). Depending on the number of teachers at each level, it may be possible to add a grade level to the team, but remember to keep the amount of participants manageable.

Vertical teams can clarify skills that are a prerequisite for the next grade, and they can strengthen and provide continuity from one grade level to the next. They agree on targets for each grade level and spend time together assessing the continuity of their programs. By doing this, they can ensure that they are aligning curricula and making learning expectations clear. Unlike grade-level teams, vertical teams do not have to meet on a weekly basis, as their work looks at the curriculum continuum and not specific daily lessons. Some vertical teams meet every few weeks and discuss an assigned topic that is common to all participants. An example of this would be sharing with the team how each member has integrated technology and instruction. At Willow Grove, kindergarten teachers and first-grade teachers met twice a year to go over targets and standards. At one of these meetings, the team discovered that both grade levels shared a few of the same targets. It doesn't make much sense for a target that requires a student to, for example, count to one hundred by ones to be taught and learned at both grade levels. If it was a target for kindergarten, then it should not be a target for first grade. Vertical teams do the same work as any other collaborative team, but they do it across grade levels. They clarify the standards and targets, they develop assessments, they look at data from the assessments, and they discuss ways to improve their instruction. DuFour, DuFour, Eaker, and Many (2006) point out, "Each teacher would have the benefit of 'two critical friends' who could offer suggestions for improvement" (p. 94).

Vertical teams can also be formed across schools and building levels. Elementary teachers could meet with middle school teachers. Second-grade and third-grade teachers could meet with the same grade-level teachers at another school in the district. This increases communication across grade levels and schools and decreases isolation. It reinforces everyone's ability to stay on the same page. Teachers become aware of the expectations at each grade level and can find support in meeting them. They can deliver a systematic program for all students. They can even discuss particular students who may need more support at the next level.

Curriculum Teams

In KCSD 96, we had teams called *job-alike, cross-school,* or *curriculum teams.* These collaborative teams focused on specific content areas of the school district's curriculum, such as literacy and mathematics. This type of structure can assist in providing clarity on broader curricular issues and learning initiatives. Administrators from each school generally place their teachers, from each grade level, on a content-area team. Then there can be teachers from different schools in the team, and everyone is represented fairly. Depending on the size of the school district, there may be more than one teacher from each school in the team. The social studies job-alike team consisted of teachers from preschool to fifth grade, as did those for mathematics, literacy, and so on. If there are four preK teachers in the district, then one could serve on the literacy team, one on mathematics, one on social studies, and so on. There may be times when there are not enough teachers to cover every content area. In that case, some teachers may serve on more than one team.

Curriculum teams ensure districtwide continuity of curriculum in each specific content area. We should expect that teachers of young children, as well as special education teachers, be included on these teams. They are part of the PLC. This enables those teachers to fully understand what mastery of a specific target and the level of rigor for that target look like. In this way, a curriculum team "deepens content knowledge and allows professionals to benefit from the wisdom of the collective *we*" (Friziellie et al., 2016, p. 23).

Leadership Teams

A school's leadership team, or guiding coalition, is the mechanism for implementing distributive leadership and expanding the impact of the school's vison and goals for student outcomes. The team ensures that the vision and goals are well established and clear to all staff. Information flows between the members of the leadership team and the rest of the PLC (the school). This free exchange reinforces a culture of feedback and open communication in the service of student learning. Teachers of young children, specialists, and special educators should all be included on a school's leadership team. This team usually consists of the team leaders from each grade level, a special education teacher or a related-services representative (or both), and a member of the intervention or problem-solving team. They meet with the school principal on a weekly basis.

For leadership teams that contain both elementary and early education teachers, when members of a leadership team come together, the concept of two separate systems in the school begins to fade away. No longer the elementary grades and the preschool: they become *our* school. PreK education and regular education staff understand that they are all responsible for the learning of every student.

The leadership team helps to build the capacity of its members. This is a process by which educators improve their knowledge and skills and other resources that they need to do their jobs more effectively. They can do this by creating conditions that help other teachers succeed—that is, continuous discussions and collaboration. Building capacity could also include coaching and mentoring from experienced leaders, learning from knowledgeable role models, and job-embedded support that nurtures teacher growth through instructional coaching and timely feedback.

Leadership teams have important conversations about building-level issues and celebrations. They discuss issues that may need to be brought forth to the whole school such as whether a new early literacy program be implemented, the school schedule, or goals for the upcoming school year. After they gather input from their peers, along with questions or decisions, they can then bring this back to the leadership team for further discussion. The leadership team may discuss issues that grade-level teams are struggling with, what teachers need more clarity about, what teams are doing well, and what the data are telling them.

One of the leadership team's most important responsibilities is to assist in establishing a school culture that focuses on student learning. They do this by modeling the behaviors, attitudes, and beliefs they want to see in their schools. In other words, they practice what they preach. The leadership team monitors any school-wide goals that are in place and helps teachers work toward achieving those goals.

Problem-Solving Teams

Every building should also have a problem-solving team, otherwise known as an intervention team. This is a multidisciplinary team that acts as the vehicle for assembling customized intervention plans for students who display the most intensive and serious learning issues. Early childhood educators and special education educators are important members of problem-solving teams. This team should also include the principal, related-service personnel, and English language supporter. The work of this team focuses on developing and implementing a pyramid of interventions to ensure that struggling students have support when they need it and not when they've fallen far enough behind to qualify for special education (Buffum, Mattos, & Malone, 2018). The team analyzes data on specific students who are struggling and provides a plan for support and interventions. Team members then support grade-level teams with information on the process of implementing and using the interventions. The problem-solving team also analyzes data of special education students and determines next steps for student support.

Now that you've gotten a sense of the many different kinds of teams and how they function in a PLC, we can go into how to organize them in the best way.

Organizing Teams

What do these teams look like for teachers of young children? Who is on the team? In many schools and districts, the leadership may need to reconsider the configuration of school teams so that they support all students. Organizing school teams to include special education teachers, preschool teachers, kindergarten teachers, and all teachers of young children supports a culture of total collaboration. Schools must also be mindful of including specialists on their teams and making sure all members have opportunities to meet, whether in person or electronically. It's important that these teams focus on the same work (that is, the essential standards for their particular grade level or program), and they must have a mutual interest in exploring the four critical questions of a PLC. Teachers can achieve more if they work together and establish meaningful learning partnerships.

The ideal makeup of a collaborative team is one that allows teachers shared responsibility for students and their learning, and one in which all team members can work together to establish goals that call for evidence of learning (Timperley & Alton-Lee, 2008). Educators learn from one another in these meetings through discussions and by applying what others have said or what they have brainstormed throughout their conversations. After discussing it with their teammates, they can begin to try new ideas in their own classrooms. "Professional development is most effective when teachers engage actively in instructional inquiry in the context of professional collaboration. . . . Research tells us that teachers need to learn the way other professionals do—continually, collaboratively, and on the job" (Wei, Darling-Hammond, Andree, Richardson, & Orphanos, 2009, p. 58).

Specialists on Teams

There are many educators who provide services to early childhood and kindergarten classrooms besides the classroom teacher. Many schools have social workers, special education teachers, speech and language therapists, reading specialists, and so on. These staff members should be included on teams.

Schools do need to be careful not to spread specialists too thin; educators should serve on no more than two teams. That would mean that the reading specialist could serve on a districtwide team and on one grade-level team. A rotation (every trimester, for example) could be established with specialists so that they can participate on different teams during the school year.

Additionally, the special education teacher, who provides services in the kindergarten classrooms, needs to be at the table with the kindergarten team. If there is a special education teacher who provides services to a preschool class, then that teacher needs to be on the preschool team. In some schools, special education teachers serve students at various grade levels. It is impossible for that teacher to attend every team meeting at every grade level. When would there be time to work with students? In their book *Yes We Can!* (Friziellie et al., 2016), the authors support redistributing caseloads for special education teachers:

> Teams restructured areas of responsibility so that one special education teacher took responsibility for resource and core content instruction for both literacy and mathematics in grades 1–2, and the other teacher took responsibility for resource and core content instruction in literacy and mathematics in grades 3–5. (p. 18)

This could easily be adjusted to include kindergarten with grades 1–2 or preschool with kindergarten and the special education teacher who provides service for students at these grade levels. This setting allows for a culture of mutual accountability. If the special education teacher is unable to attend these meetings, it becomes the responsibility of one teacher to communicate the details of the meeting. A great communication piece for the whole team is to record the minutes through an electronic system, such as Google Docs (www.google.com/docs).

Don't underestimate the importance of specialists being part of these teams and being present at these meetings. Their knowledge of instructional practices is strong, and they can share a lot of differentiation strategies with the team. The occupational therapist in my school, for example, had a lot to offer the team in the development of students' fine and gross motor skills. It is also important that specialists and the special education teacher all understand the grade-level targets for the students on their caseloads. Remember that in a PLC, there is shared

Electronic Teams

If it is not possible to physically meet with your team members, another option would be to establish an electronic team. Electronic teams have many resources available to them, such as Skype (https://skype.com/en), Zoom (https://zoom.us), or GoToMeeting (https://gotomeeting.com). Figure 3.1 is a list of digital resources for electronic teams.

Four Digital Resources for Electronic Learning Teams

There are new digital tools that can facilitate progress-driven work around any collaborative task. This collection of four useful resources may help get your electronic learning team off of the ground.

Conducting Synchronous Meetings

Like more traditional teams, electronic learning teams should be engaging in regularly scheduled synchronous meetings that are focused on the kinds of instructional practices that have a positive impact on student learning.

 Google Hangouts

While at first glance it may appear to be a nontraditional option for educators, Google Hangouts (http://hangouts.google.com) is probably the best tool for electronic teams trying to schedule synchronous meetings simply because it allows up to nine people to join a conversation at one time, allows participants to share their screens and collaborate around shared documents, and is completely free. Synchronous meetings held in Google+ Hangouts can also be easily recorded and posted online for future reference.

Creating Shared Documents

Regardless of how they are structured, professional learning teams generate a ton of shared documents: common assessments, sets of essential outcomes, potential lessons, and exemplars of student work, for example. For electronic learning teams, services that allow members to work—synchronously or asynchronously—on these kinds of documents are essential.

FIGURE 3.1: Digital resources for electronic learning teams.

continued →

Creating Shared Documents

 Google Drive

Google Drive (http://drive.google.com) is a service that allows groups of users to collaborate around Word documents, spreadsheets, presentations, and forms in online spaces. Edits appear automatically, making it possible for team members to work simultaneously on the same document. Teams can then download final products in more traditional formats—Word documents, PDF files, PowerPoint presentations—or post them directly to the web.

Warehousing Team Content

The most efficient learning teams develop systems, structures, and spaces for storing their shared content. When resources are carefully organized and readily available to members, learning teams thrive.

 PBworks

PBworks (https://plans.pbworks.com/academic) is a wiki service that offers free basic accounts to educators. *Wikis*—easy-to-edit websites—are a fantastic solution for electronic learning teams looking to create warehouses of shared content because they require little digital skill to master. As long as members can create basic documents and add attachments to emails, they can edit a team wiki.

Tackling Multiple Tasks

For many electronic learning teams, a priority in selecting digital tools is finding services that address multiple collaborative tasks at one time. These all-in-one homes are valuable primarily because they provide many electronic opportunities with a single password.

 Edmodo

Edmodo (www.edmodo.com), a popular free service that has been widely embraced by educators, offers users the ability to carry on asynchronous conversations, conduct group polls, maintain a shared calendar, and create warehouses of team documents. While Edmodo doesn't offer synchronous conversation or shared document creation options, it's popular with educators who often begin using the service to create online homes for their students, too.

Source: Adapted from Ferriter, Graham, & Wight, 2013.

*Visit **go.SolutionTree.com/PLCbooks** for a free reproducible version of this figure.*

Electronic teams do the same core work as teams that meet in person. They investigate their practice, develop common assessments, look at student data, and plan instruction. You don't have to be sitting right next to your colleagues to have relevant conversations about the students you teach. What's essential is to find a way to have those conversations to achieve equity for all students who attend the same grade in a district, whether that means occasionally traveling across the district or setting up an online meeting. Teachers of these students must still focus on and agree to the same targets or standards. The learning standards should not be different from one school to another in a district, nor should they be different from one classroom to another.

Early childhood educators may be asking themselves, "But how do I make collaborative teams work in my specific situation?" The next section discusses teams in the context of early childhood education and how teachers of young children can make time for teams, ensure they are doing the right work, and use team tools to create structures for effective teamwork.

Collaborative Teams for Early Childhood Educators

Collaborative teams are the lifeblood of PLCs. In *Learning by Doing*, a collaborative team is defined as "a group of people working together *interdependently* to achieve a *common goal* for which members are held *mutually accountable*" (DuFour et al., 2016, p. 42). It is kind of like getting everyone rowing in the same direction. Teachers are working together toward a common purpose—student learning. DuFour and Fullan (2013) determine that when educators have clarity and support they are better equipped to succeed at what they are asked to do. They explain the correlation between clarity of purpose and effective schools. Members of a team help clarify what students need to learn, plan more effective lessons, assess student work, and solve common problems of teaching and learning. When teachers collaborate, it allows them to plan for their own professional development, which becomes highly relevant to their day-to-day work. Teachers' skills improve, and students excel. Collaboration also allows for shared leadership, because staff members have input on decision making. No one teacher has all the skills, knowledge, and time to meet the needs of every student in his or her class. Teachers in teams must rely on one another to achieve success for all students. Relying on each other creates a sense of responsibility among team members. This strengthens the team and helps teachers better understand the content and meaning of the curriculum. Teachers mentor each other and challenge each other to use best education practices.

This all sounds great, but many early childhood educators are not used to it. They may have never spent time discussing content or student learning. Many early childhood classroom teachers go into their classroom, shut the door, and teach—and this is what they have done for many years. There has been a tradition of isolation. Schools consisted of many independent islands, especially for little ones. Author and psychologist Seymour B. Sarason (1996) asserts that teachers have always been isolated, especially special education teachers and teachers of young children, therefore they created their own islands. Researchers have identified several factors that lead to teacher burnout, a common thread being the lack of relationships with peers (Schlichte, Yssel, & Merbler, 2005).

Many times, special educators, along with teachers of young children, are not only isolated but segregated physically in the building. They get a room, area, or cubbyhole that was left over. Many of their classrooms are situated far away from the general education classrooms. They may even sit alone in the teacher's lounge, feeling that they have nothing in common with the elementary teachers. They are not required (or invited) to attend staff meetings because the conversations don't pertain to them. Some teachers who have been operating in isolation for years teach the way they believe works best. They keep to themselves, they hoard materials, and they seldom buy into change. Early childhood teachers tend to be less familiar with how to set up collaborative opportunities and how to facilitate them because of the isolation they may have experienced when they began teaching. In some cases, they may not have participated on a school team because they are the only early childhood teacher in the building.

These are the reasons why early childhood leaders and administrators need a deeper understanding of how collaborative structures work. PLCs reject teacher isolation and open the doors to discover new ways for teachers to improve their craft through collaboration, creating a culture of mutual, supportive, ongoing learning (Hamos et al., 2009). Teachers feel less isolated in PLCs, and they experience higher morale. PLCs focus teachers on student work and achievement data which is more satisfying, so teachers are then more effective (Basileo, 2016). Research analyst Lindsey Devers Basileo (2016) also notes that better teacher morale is highly correlated with working to improve student learning rather than discussing student behavior, building issues, or school activities. According to a report from a Learning Sciences International research team, "Participation in high functioning professional learning communities (PLCs) improves teacher morale, and higher levels of teacher morale are significantly correlated with practices that drive student achievement" (Meyer, 2016).

Due to possible isolation and physical classroom segregation of preK programs, many teachers of young children may initially be reluctant to give up their autonomy and individuality to become interdependent. There may be barriers that prevent them from embracing a culture of collaboration, such as differing teaching styles or behavior management philosophies. They may fear change or have issues with trust. Collaborating with other teachers gives teachers an opportunity to explore those differences. Remember, your colleagues are your best source for professional development. Use them and their ideas.

It's important to overcome old attitudes about teams. Collaborating and sharing ideas and teaching strategies with one another might be something that early childhood teachers have rarely, if ever, done. Even if they did share, it was never the good stuff. Sometimes teachers of the same grade level might get together to decide what should be on next year's school supply list, but they never really relied on or learned from one another. But in a PLC, it is no longer about the leader and the followers. Everyone has a voice. As early educators begin to work together, they will start to find meaning in their communal work by accepting responsibility for their own growth, developing a group identity and norms, and using conflict to solve problems. By openly addressing differences and opposing opinions, teachers can then begin to search for resolutions that would allow all stakeholders to move forward. Conflict is a tool that helps raise and address problems. When teachers had very different opinions on what literacy curriculum to use at Willow Grove, the team structures we had in place enabled them to focus their energy on the issue at hand. They were able to recognize and benefit from their differences.

Early childhood teachers need to abandon the tradition of isolation, step out of their communities of practice, and discover relationships with other preK teachers. Teams can consist of all preK teachers in the building, at other buildings, or in nearby school districts. Even when there is only one early childhood teacher in a building—*a singleton*—there are ways to collaborate with other educators. I present tools for this later in the chapter (page 64).

Early childhood teams can also be made up of a classroom teacher, special education teacher, speech-language pathologist, physical therapist, school psychologist, and others. A culture of privacy and noninterference can no longer be the status quo (Schmoker, 2001). Just because you have a classroom aide doesn't mean that you are not isolated. You are! We increase capacity when we work together.

There is much research to support high-performing teams and the impact they have on student learning. According to DuFour, DuFour, and Eaker (2008), teams are the engine that drives school improvement. Sparks (2013) asserts that high-functioning teams are essential to continuous school improvement. They are the force behind superior teaching and learning as they help to clearly articulate what learning looks like for their students. Schools must embed the collaborative team process into their routines "to ensure that they co-labor in a coordinated and systemic process to support the students they serve" (DuFour, 2011, p. 59). Collaborative teams have great power, as they are the vehicles that improve student achievement. Teacher teams improve the quality and equity of student learning. Collaborative teams in schools engage in discussions around best practices in teaching and learning such as curriculum, instruction, and assessment. Their discussions are grounded in evidence and analysis rather than opinion or belief in something simply because it is something that they've always done. Teams foster collective responsibility for student success. They practice open and honest communication.

Making Time for Teams to Meet

Professional development is crucial to teacher growth and student learning and should therefore be built into the workday and be part of a teacher's professional responsibility (DuFour, 2015). This means that schools must embed time for collaboration into their routine practices and specifically structure teachers' work schedules around the time. The result is authentic collaboration. Each school must protect this time and not permit teachers to use it for other tasks, such as calling a parent, making copies of lessons, and so on. Tolerating these uses of the time means the meetings will not be effective.

Time for team meetings should be built into the school's weekly schedule just as art, music, or physical education are. Randomly choosing times and dates to meet is not sufficient. Team time should also occur during the school day, so that teachers do not have to use personal time to collaborate. The school administrator or leadership team should embed team meetings into the schedule. Some schools schedule team time when there is an early dismissal. The resource "Making Time for Collaboration" (www.allthingsplc.info/files/uploads/makingtimeforcollaboration.pdf) is very useful.

Education professor Linda Darling-Hammond (2009) discusses results from a report by the National Staff Development Council stating that when teachers routinely collaborate, their levels of trust are high and they much more efficiently share new learning practices. Many times, the familiar school schedule must be thrown out the window in favor of a completely new, different, and original schedule.

Teacher leaders, along with the school principal, may have to get creative to provide this necessary time for teachers to collaborate. A fresh set of eyes can be very helpful when looking at a school's schedule. Find the teacher who is very organized and have him or her look. At Willow Grove, I had a team of teachers create the schedule. They set up a huge table in the learning center (our library or media center) with lots of chart paper, markers, and sticky notes and recreated the status quo.

Some great examples of school schedules that provide time for collaboration are available on the AllThingsPLC website (www.allthingsplc.info/evidence). In particular, check Cheshire Elementary School in Delaware, Ohio (www.allthingsplc

.info/files/uploads/ces-16-17-schedule--revised-august-15.pdf), and Big Sandy Elementary in Tuscaloosa, Alabama (www.allthingsplc.info/files/uploads/master-schedule-9095.pdf), to find examples of their building schedules. At Willow Grove, teachers meet when their students are in the charge of other professionals in the building, such as during physical education, learning centers, or even recess. Some early childhood programs are four days a week. The fifth day might be used for home visits, paperwork, IEP meetings, or professional development. This is the perfect time for a weekly one-hour meeting. Schedule it! Although regular team time should take place during the school day, there may also be times when teams meet over the summer to work on larger projects, such as writing common assessments or developing rubrics for assessments. Some school districts use early release time or staff development time for teams to meet. Even school institute days have been used to give teams time to collaborate. In KCSD 96 in Buffalo Grove, Illinois, there were times when teachers were released from teaching to do the work. Whatever way it is accomplished, team time is a vital and important piece of a PLC.

Figure 3.2 (pages 52–55) is an example of a schedule from Aspen Early Learning Center in Fremont County School District No. 25 in Wyoming. It sets time every week for a team meeting and includes specifics such as staff names and instructional times. This schedule groups classes together and assigns staff members to teams. Elements like color coding can further enhance a schedule like this.

Focusing on the Right Things

All teams must focus on the right things to be successful and to feel they are using their time wisely. All teachers feel that there is not enough time in the school day to get everything done, but it can be even more daunting for preK teachers. Many teachers who work with young children are dealing with severe time constraints. Their programs may only be three hours a day or only four days a week. They commonly feel that there is not enough time in each day to accomplish what's necessary to ensure that all their students learn at high levels. Spending time at a meeting without accomplishing anything can be very frustrating. We cannot spend time focusing on the wrong things. Teams need to focus on the four critical questions of a PLC (DuFour et al., 2016).

1. What do we want students to know and be able to do?
2. How will we know if they have learned it?
3. What will we do if they have not learned it?
4. What will we do if they already know it?

Teachers 1, 2, 3

Time	Monday, Tuesday, Thursday, Friday	Wednesday
8:00–8:05	Mathematics	PLC
8:05–8:10		
8:10–8:15		
8:15–8:20		
8:20–8:25		
8:25–8:30		
8:30–8:35	Writing	
8:35–8:40		
8:40–8:45		
8:45–8:50		Writing
8:50–8:55		
8:55–9:00		
9:00–9:05	Reading	
9:05–9:10		
9:10–9:15		
9:15–9:20		
9:20–9:25		
9:25–9:30		
9:30–9:35	Recess	
9:35–9:40		
9:40–9:45		
9:45–9:50		

Teachers 3, 4, 5, 6, 7, 8

Time	Monday, Tuesday, Thursday, Friday	Wednesday
8:00–8:05	Science, Social Studies, Calendar	PLC
8:05–8:10		
8:10–8:15		
8:15–8:20		
8:20–8:25		
8:25–8:30		
8:30–8:35		
8:35–8:40		
8:40–8:45		
8:45–8:50	Reader's Workshop	
8:50–8:55		
8:55–9:00		
9:00–9:05		
9:05–9:10		
9:10–9:15		
9:15–9:20		
9:20–9:25		
9:25–9:30		
9:30–9:35		
9:35–9:40		
9:40–9:45	Recess	
9:45–9:50		

Teachers 9, 10, 11, 12, 13

Time	Monday, Tuesday, Thursday, Friday	Wednesday
8:00–8:05	Science, Social Studies, Calendar	PLC
8:05–8:10		
8:10–8:15		
8:15–8:20		
8:20–8:25		
8:25–8:30		
8:30–8:35		
8:35–8:40		
8:40–8:45		
8:45–8:50	Reader's Workshop	
8:50–8:55		
8:55–9:00		
9:00–9:05		
9:05–9:10		
9:10–9:15		
9:15–9:20		
9:20–9:25		
9:25–9:30		
9:30–9:35		
9:35–9:40		
9:40–9:45	Read Aloud	
9:45–9:50		

Collaborative Teams in Early Childhood Programs

Teachers 1, 2, 3		
	Monday, Tuesday, Thursday, Friday	Wednesday
9:50–9:55	Reading	
9:55–10:00		
10:00–10:05		
10:05–10:10		
10:10–10:15		
10:15–10:20		
10:20–10:25	Word Study	
10:25–10:30		
10:30–10:35		
10:35–10:40		
10:40–10:45		
10:45–10:50		
10:50–10:55		
10:55–11:00		
11:00–11:05	Lunch	
11:05–11:10		
11:10–11:15		
11:15–11:20		
11:20–11:25	Lunch, Recess	
11:25–11:30		

Teachers 3, 4, 5, 6, 7, 8		
	Monday, Tuesday, Thursday, Friday	Wednesday
9:50–9:55	Recess	
9:55–10:00	Read Aloud	
10:00–10:05		
10:05–10:10		
10:10–10:15	Reading and Mathematics Intervention	
10:15–10:20		
10:20–10:25	Reading and Mathematics Intervention	
10:25–10:30		
10:30–10:35		
10:35–10:40		
10:40–10:45		
10:45–10:50		
10:50–10:55		
10:55–11:00	Writing	
11:00–11:05		
11:05–11:10		
11:10–11:15		
11:15–11:20		
11:20–11:25		
11:25–11:30		

Teachers 9, 10, 11, 12, 13		
	Monday, Tuesday, Thursday, Friday	Wednesday
9:50–9:55	Read Aloud	
9:55–10:00	Recess	
10:00–10:05		
10:05–10:10		
10:10–10:15	Reading and Mathematics Intervention	
10:15–10:20		
10:20–10:25	Reading and Mathematics Intervention	
10:25–10:30		
10:30–10:35		
10:35–10:40		
10:40–10:45		
10:45–10:50		
10:50–10:55		
10:55–11:00	Writing	
11:00–11:05		
11:05–11:10		
11:10–11:15		
11:15–11:20		
11:20–11:25		
11:25–11:30		

FIGURE 3.2: Aspen Early Learning Center schedule.

continued →

Teachers 1, 2, 3

Time	Monday, Tuesday, Thursday, Friday	Wednesday
11:30–11:35	Lunch, Recess	
11:35–11:40	Specials	
11:40–11:45		
11:45–11:50		
11:50–11:55		
11:55–12:00		
12:00–12:05		
12:05–12:10		Specials
12:10–12:15		
12:15–12:20		
12:20–12:25		
12:25–12:30		
12:30–12:35		
12:35–12:40	Science and Social Studies	Science and Social Studies
12:40–12:45		
12:45–12:50		
12:50–12:55		
12:55–1:00		
1:00–1:05		
1:05–1:10	Mathematics	Mathematics
1:10–1:15		

Teachers 3, 4, 5, 6, 7, 8

Time	Monday, Tuesday, Thursday, Friday	Wednesday
11:30–11:35	Lunch—Teachers 6, 7, 8; Recess—Teachers 4, 5	Lunch—Teachers 6, 7, 8; Recess—Teachers 4, 5
11:35–11:40		
11:40–11:45		
11:45–11:50		
11:50–11:55	Lunch—Teachers 4, 5; Recess—Teachers 6, 7, 8	Lunch—Teachers 4, 5; Recess—Teachers 6, 7, 8
11:55–12:00		
12:00–12:05		
12:05–12:10		
12:10–12:15	Word Study: Phonics and Handwriting	
12:15–12:20		
12:20–12:25		
12:25–12:30		
12:30–12:35		
12:35–12:40		
12:40–12:45		
12:45–12:50		
12:50–12:55	Mathematics	
12:55–1:00		
1:00–1:05		
1:05–1:10		
1:10–1:15		

Teachers 9, 10, 11, 12, 13

Time	Monday, Tuesday, Thursday, Friday	Wednesday
11:30–11:35	Word Study: Phonics and Handwriting	
11:35–11:40		
11:40–11:45		
11:45–11:50		
11:50–11:55		
11:55–12:00		
12:00–12:05		
12:05–12:10		
12:10–12:15	Lunch—Teachers 10, 11, 12; Recess—Teachers 9, 13	Lunch—Teachers 10, 11, 12; Recess—Teachers 9, 13
12:15–12:20		
12:20–12:25		
12:25–12:30		
12:30–12:35	Recess—Teachers 10, 11, 12; Lunch—Teachers 9, 13	Recess—Teachers 10, 11, 12; Lunch—Teachers 9, 13
12:35–12:40		
12:40–12:45		
12:45–12:50		
12:50–12:55	Specials	
12:55–1:00		
1:00–1:05		
1:05–1:10		
1:10–1:15		

Collaborative Teams in Early Childhood Programs

Teachers 1, 2, 3	Monday, Tuesday, Thursday, Friday	Wednesday
1:15–1:20	Mathematics	Mathematics
1:20–1:25		
1:25–1:30		
1:30–1:35		
1:35–1:40	Recess	Recess
1:40–1:45		
1:45–1:50	Handwriting	Handwriting
1:50–1:55		
1:55–2:00		
2:00–2:05		
2:05–2:10	Intervention	Intervention
2:10–2:15		
2:15–2:20		
2:20–2:25		
2:25–2:30		
2:30–2:35		
2:35–2:40		
2:40–2:45	Read Aloud	Read Aloud
2:45–2:50		
2:50–2:55		
2:55–3:00		

Teachers 3, 4, 5, 6, 7, 8	Monday, Tuesday, Thursday, Friday	Wednesday
1:15–1:20	Mathematics	
1:20–1:25		
1:25–1:30		
1:30–1:35		
1:35–1:40		
1:40–1:45		
1:45–1:50		
1:50–1:55		
1:55–2:00	Specials	
2:00–2:05		
2:05–2:10		
2:10–2:15		
2:15–2:20		
2:20–2:25		
2:25–2:30	Specials	
2:30–2:35		
2:35–2:40		
2:40–2:45		
2:45–2:50		
2:50–2:55		
2:55–3:00		

Teachers 9, 10, 11, 12, 13	Monday, Tuesday, Thursday, Friday	Wednesday
1:15–1:20	Specials	
1:20–1:25	Specials	
1:25–1:30		
1:30–1:35		
1:35–1:40		
1:40–1:45		
1:45–1:50		
1:50–1:55	Mathematics	
1:55–2:00		
2:00–2:05		
2:05–2:10		
2:10–2:15		
2:15–2:20		
2:20–2:25		
2:25–2:30		
2:30–2:35		
2:35–2:40		
2:40–2:45		
2:45–2:50		
2:50–2:55		
2:55–3:00		

Source: Adapted from AllThingsPLC, n.d.b.

Meetings cannot be about field trips, supply lists, or holiday parties. We can accomplish so much of that type of work and those conversations in emails, memos, and so on. The work of the team must revolve around the four critical questions as it develops essential standards and targets for students, forms and refines assessment practices, discusses individual students and their needs, and looks at data and analyzes the results. This in turn drives instruction.

The team determines when learning will take place and agrees on pacing. It must concentrate on essential tools, such as pacing guides, to help codify the critical questions. Figure 3.3 is an example of a kindergarten pacing guide for mathematics.

These types of guides should be simple: easy to read and understand. They are directly connected to the four critical questions. Essential standards, what the students are to learn and be able to do (critical question 1), are 3.0 targets. A 4.0 target identifies how teachers can extend or enrich a student's learning if he or she has already met the 3.0 target (critical question 4). Achievement of a 2.0 target indicates that a student needs more time and practice to be successful (critical question 3). The pacing guide also notes when to teach and assess each target (critical question 2). This information should be publicly accessible for parents and students at every grade level. It is important for families to know what their children need to know and be able to do to be successful at their grade level.

Kindergarten Bridges Mathematics Pacing Guide 2018–2019

4.0 Target	3.0 Target	2.0 Target	Trimester and Unit
Counting and Cardinality			
Count to 100 by fives (starting from zero and given a number other than zero or five)	K.CC.1.1: Count to 100 by ones.	Count to 50 by ones.	Trimester 1 and 2 Trimester 3 May Number Corner for mastery
Count to 100 by tens, beginning at numbers that are not decade numbers; 33, 43, 53, and so on.	K.CC.1.2: Count to 100 by tens.	Inconsistently count to 100 by tens.	Trimester 3 May Number Corner

FIGURE 3.3: Sample kindergarten mathematics pacing guide.

4.0 Target	3.0 Target	2.0 Target	Trimester and Unit
Counting and Cardinality			
Count forward by ones between 100 and 120 beginning with a given number.	K.CC.2: Count forward beginning from a given number within the known sequence (instead of having to begin at one).	Count forward beginning with a number other than one with a running start.	Trimester 2 January Number Corner
Does Not Extend	K.CC.3: Write numbers from zero to twenty. Represent a number of objects with a written numeral 0–20 (with zero representing a count of no objects).	Write numbers from zero to twenty; or represent a number of objects with a written numeral 0–20.	Trimester 3 March Number Corner
Does Not Extend	K.CC.4a: When counting objects (at least 20), say the number names in the standard order, pairing each object with one and only one number name and each number name with one and only one object (1:1 correspondence).	Count less than twenty objects with 1:1 correspondence.	Trimester 1 and Trimester 2 January Number Corner for mastery
Does Not Extend	K.CC.4b: Understand that the last number name said tells the number of objects counted (up to 20). The number of objects is the same regardless of their arrangement or the order in which they were counted.	Inconsistently names the last number counted or does not automatically recall the quantity; needs to recount after prompted	Trimester 1 and Trimester 2 January Number Corner for mastery
Does Not Extend	K.CC.4c: Understand that each successive number name refers to a quantity that is one larger.	Names the next number name after given an amount (up to ten)	Trimester 3 March Number Corner

continued →

4.0 Target	3.0 Target	2.0 Target	Trimester and Unit
Counting and Cardinality			
Identify which of two given amounts is greater than, less than, or equal to, and by how many.	K.CC.6: Identify whether the number of objects in one group is greater than, less than, or equal to the number of objects in another group.	Inconsistently identify whether the number of objects in one group is greater than, less than, or equal to the number of objects in another group.	Trimester 2 and Trimester 3 March Number Corner
Identify which of two given numerals within 100 is greater than, less than, or equal to the other and use inequality signs in an equation (for example, 34 > 27).	K.CC.7: Compare two numbers between 1 and 10 presented as written numerals.	Compare two numbers between 1 and 10 presented as written numerals with a visual present (for example, pictures, manipulatives, and so on).	Trimester 3 March Number Corner
Operations and Algebraic Thinking			
Solve multistep word problems using addition and subtraction within twenty.	K.OA.2: Solve addition and subtraction word problems, and add and subtract within ten.	Represent addition and subtraction with objects, fingers, mental images, drawings, sounds, acting out situations, verbal explanations, expressions, or equations.	Trimester 3 May Number Corner
Does Not Extend	K.OA.3: Decompose numbers less than or equal to ten into pairs in more than one way, and record each decomposition by a drawing or equation (for example, 5 = 2 + 3 and 5 = 4 + 1).	Decompose numbers less than or equal to ten in one way, and record each decomposition by a drawing or equation.	Trimester 3 May Number Corner

4.0 Target	3.0 Target	2.0 Target	Trimester and Unit
Operations and Algebraic Thinking			
Find and record the missing addend in a sum within ten; 3 + ___ = 7, ___ + 6 = 8.	K.OA.4: For any number from 1 to 9, find the number that makes 10 when added to the given number, and record the answer with a drawing or equation.	Inconsistently find the number that makes 10 when added to the given number, and record the answer with a drawing or equation.	Trimester 3 March Number Corner
Fluently add and subtract within 10 (1.OA.6.2 and 6.3).	K.OA.5: Fluently add and subtract within 5.	Inconsistently add and subtract within 5.	Trimester 2 (developing) Trimester 3 May Number Corner
Number and Operations in Base Ten			
Compose and decompose and record two-digit numbers into tens and ones (1.NBT.2).	K.NBT.1: Compose and decompose numbers from 11 to 19 into ten ones and some further ones, and record each composition or decomposition by a drawing or equation (for example, 18 = 10 + 8); understand that these numbers are composed of ten ones and one, two, three, four, five, six, seven, eight, or nine ones.	When given a unit of ten and some ones, count one by one to determine the quantity from 11 to 19 (does not understand that numbers are composed of ten ones and some more ones).	Trimester 3 May Number Corner
Measurement and Data			
Classify, count, and sort objects into three or more student-created categories.	K.MD.3: Classify objects into given categories; count the numbers of objects in each category and sort the categories by count.	Determine if an object fits into a given category.	Trimester 2 Unit 5; January Number Corner

continued →

4.0 Target	3.0 Target	2.0 Target	Trimester and Unit
Geometry			
Use comparative language to point out a difference and a similarity between 2-D shapes.	K.G.1.1: Describe 2-D objects in the environment, regardless of their orientation or size, using names of shapes (square, circle, triangle, rectangle, rhombus, trapezoid, hexagon).	Identify 2-D objects, regardless of their orientation or size, when given a choice (square, circle, triangle, rectangle, rhombus, trapezoid, hexagon).	Trimester 2 Unit 5; January Number Corner
Use comparative language to point out a difference and a similarity between 3-D shapes.	K.G.1.2: Describe 3-D objects in the environment, regardless of their orientation or size, using names of shapes (cube, sphere, cone cylinder).	Identify 3-D objects, regardless of their orientation or size, when given a choice (cube, sphere, cone cylinder).	Trimester 3 Unit 6
Does Not Extend	K.G.1.3: Describe the relative positions of objects using terms such as above, below, beside, in front of, behind, and next to.	Identify relative positions of objects when given a choice of terms such as above, below, beside, in front of, behind, and next to.	Trimester 3 January Number Corner

Source for standards: Adapted from NGA & CCSSO, 2010b.
Source: ©2018 by Kildeer Countryside CCSD 96. Adapted with permission.

An early childhood pacing guide from Kildeer Countryside CCSD 96 illustrates the targets that the students must learn and be able to do in language arts (see figure 3.4).

Early Childhood Language Arts Standards 2018-2019

4.0 Expectation	3.0 Target	2.0 Expectation	T1	T2	T3
See Rubric	1.A.ECb: Respond appropriately to questions from others.	See Rubric	X	X	X
See Rubric	1.B.ECb: With teacher assistance, participate in collaborative conversations with diverse partners (e.g., peers and adults in both small and large groups) about age-appropriate topics and texts.	See Rubric	X	X	X
See Rubric	1.E.ECc: With teacher assistance, use new words acquired through conversations and book-sharing experiences.	See Rubric	X	X	X
See Rubric	1.E.ECd: With teacher assistance, explore word relationships to understand the concepts represented by common categories of words (e.g., food, clothing, vehicles).	See Rubric	X	X	X
Goal 2					
4.0 Expectation	3.0 Target	2.0 Expectation	T1	T2	T3
N/A	2.A.ECa: Engage in book-sharing experiences with purpose and understanding.	See Rubric	X	X	X
Goal 3					
4.0 Expectation	3.0 Target	2.0 Expectation	T1	T2	T3
See Rubric	3.B.ECa: With teacher assistance, identify basic similarities and differences in pictures and information found in two texts on the same topic.	See Rubric	X	X	X
Goal 4					
4.0 Expectation	3.0 Target	2.0 Expectation	T1	T2	T3
N/A	4.A.ECb: Begin to follow words from left to right, top to bottom, and page by page.	See Rubric	X	X	X
See Rubric	4.B.ECb: Recognize and name some upper and lowercase letters of the alphabet, especially those in own name.	See Rubric	X	X	X
N/A	4.D.ECa: Recognize own name and common signs and labels in the environment.	See Rubric	X	X	X

FIGURE 3.4: Sample early childhood English language arts pacing guide. *continued →*

Goal 5					
4.0 Expectation	3.0 Target	2.0 Expectation	T1	T2	T3
See Rubric	5.A.ECb: Use scribbles, letter-like forms, or letters and words to represent written language.	See Rubric	X	X	X
See Rubric	5.B.ECc: With teacher assistance, use a combination of drawing, dictating, or writing to narrate a single event and provide a reaction to what happened.	See Rubric	X	X	X

Source for standards: Illinois State Board of Education, 2013.
Source: ©2018 by Kildeer Countryside CCSD 96. Used with permission.

The Kildeer schedule states in what trimester teachers will teach and assess each target. For example, the developmental expectation for a student between the ages of three and four is to recognize his or her name in print. Some students may achieve this before they are three, and some may not until they are closer to four. Preschool teachers work on this in a variety of ways during the school day and all through the school year. Since they are constantly teaching this target, they are continually assessing this skill through observation. If a student is not able to recognize his or her name in print as they approach four, then the teacher can provide more support for the individual student. Generally, these classrooms have mixed-age students, and therefore many of the targets are taught on a continual basis due to individual developmental levels.

Teams build shared knowledge and make decisions by reaching consensus. Consensus is necessary to ensure that all team members are engaged in the decision-making process and support the decisions of the group. Teams achieve consensus when all points of view are not only heard but solicited, and the will of the group is evident even to those who oppose it. It also means that those who oppose it will not be having their own meetings in the parking lot after school but will publicly support the decision. A simple fist-to-five activity can lead to a decision (see figure 3.5).

Teams commit to achieving the results they desire. School environments need to be places where trusting individuals are committed to asking the right questions that will ensure positive education outcomes for all students. As we established earlier, it is the purpose of teachers to ensure that their students learn at high levels. The only way we can ensure this is to look at the results of our teaching and find meaning in those results as a team. We accomplish this through frequent

\multicolumn{2}{c}{**Fist-to-Five Ratings**}
\multicolumn{2}{l}{Each time our team comes together to make important decisions, we will use fist-to-five ratings as a strategy to identify our levels of collective consensus. When deciding on the rating that you will give to each decision, consider the following descriptors.}
Rating	**Descriptor**
5	**Why didn't we make this decision sooner?** This idea is great, and we've got the capacity to make it happen without investing a ton of new effort. I've fallen in love with this idea, and I'm willing to lead any efforts to make it become reality.
4	**This is a decision that I completely support.** I really believe that it aligns well with our school's mission and just know it is going to help our students to succeed. I'm willing to move forward and am also willing to put some time, energy, and effort into helping to make this happen.
3	**I believe in this decision, but question our timing.** I think this is a great idea and definitely something worth pursuing, I'm just not sure that this is the right time to move forward. I'm excited to see where this decision goes, but I think we should set it aside for now. I won't be opposed if others invest energy into making this happen, but I can't promise that I'll help.
2	**You know, I'm not totally comfortable with this decision, but I can see it has merit.** I'm willing to move forward with the decision as it currently stands—and I won't put any barriers in our team's way as we work to make this happen—but I'm probably going to need some practical and philosophical support before I'll completely embrace this action.
1	**This is a decision that I have strong reservations about.** While I can see some potential in taking this action, there are several things that we need to consider before I can be comfortable with this. Can we do a bit more talking before moving forward, please?
Fist	**There is no way I could possibly support this decision.** In fact, I think that supporting this decision would be irresponsible because it doesn't align with our school's mission and may even harm our students. We shouldn't even consider this action.
\multicolumn{2}{l}{What thoughts do you have about the decision we are making? Are there any key ideas that we are forgetting to consider? What steps are we going to have to take before we can move forward?}

Source: Adapted from Graham & Ferriter, 2010.

FIGURE 3.5: Fist-to-five ratings.

common formative assessments and by analyzing the data from those assessments. For teachers of young children, assessment can be very different for their students than it is for older students. However, early education teachers must develop a way to be sure that their students have learned the skills they need to learn. If you are not certain that a student knows all the letters of the alphabet, how can you be confident that he or she will learn the letter sounds? Teachers must openly share their students' performance and reflect on their practice with trusted colleagues. Gaining trust does not happen overnight. As a principal, when I first decided to share individual teachers' data, I did it without identifying classrooms or teacher names; I reported the student data only. I was not confident that my staff had enough trust or self-assurance to see their results compared to their peers. They were still doing a lot of things in isolation, and we were not really collaborating as teams at that point. It was much easier to see the data and not single anyone out as the one whose students were struggling. I felt that they may take it as a personal affront to their teaching ability. My staff were not ready for that. Of course, teachers recognized their own classes, but this gave them an opportunity to see the results of the other classrooms. In time, the staff did begin to identify their classrooms to one another and did discuss their results, but this is something that cannot be forced. We eventually moved to public display and discussions of teachers' data and classroom results.

Looking at classroom assessment data is the only way for teachers to see "tangible evidence their students are acquiring the knowledge, skills, and dispositions essential to their future success" (DuFour et al., 2006, p. 117). Initially, it may be difficult to share assessment results with your colleagues, but it is a powerful way to improve instruction. Being results-oriented is the way to eliminate the achievement gap. When teachers have proof (accurate information) that a student is not learning, they should feel compelled to act responsibly and rectify it. Assessments guide teachers to act if a student is not learning. Assessments not only provide educators with critical information about a student's learning but can be an important piece of information to share with parents. I will discuss assessments for young children in chapter 5 (page 87).

Using Team Tools

Team members must be able to have frank, direct conversations while asking and answering challenging questions. There are always lots of discussions around what is developmentally appropriate for young children in the area of assessment. Many educators have differing views and very strong feelings in this area. Teams face difficult discussions about goals for their students who are severely impaired. Determining behavior strategies for difficult students can also lend itself to lively conversations.

Teams can use tools such as norms and agendas to create structures that make such conversations safe. These challenging conversations can be a new experience for early childhood teachers, yet they must take place to ensure equity and to allow everyone's voice to be heard. When the structures are in place to include everyone's voice, teams become more efficient and put their time to good use, and teachers develop trust as they work together and honor the commitments they have made to one another and to their students. Eric Twadell (2016) writes in his blog:

> We build trust by working together in collaborative teams, by sharing resources, by planning together, by observing each other's classes, developing common assessments, examining data, and reflecting with one another on how we might support students more effectively and improve our instructional practice. Trust is not built outside of the work of our teams, trust is built in our teams as we are doing the work.

Trust will take time to build, so give it the time it needs.

Teams should build in space for listening and give members permission to listen without responding. Promote in-depth, insightful conversations about teaching young children and about their learning. To govern behavior during meetings, clarify expectations, and create that sense of safety I spoke about, teams identify their norms. *Norms* are the ground rules for how teams function and operate. They are the commitments or promises that teacher teams make to create a comfortable environment for their education discussions. Norms help to build trust and hold people accountable, and they can have a big impact on team cohesiveness and performance. Established norms at meetings such as *being prepared and professional and listening to others* and *getting to the meeting on time and staying on task*, help team members monitor and manage behavior.

Before we established our own norms at Willow Grove, I remember meetings in which teachers were cutting out snowflakes or checking their email. We needed to develop a norm within our own building to address this. Many times, people rolled in late and just asked for updates. That does not demonstrate professionalism and is unfair to those who are on time. Other schools or teams may have different issues to address in their norms. Although a team can pause and set norms at any time, it is ideal to set norms at the beginning of a group's work together. If you don't set norms at the beginning, you will have more difficulty dialing back problematic behavior when it becomes obvious. Once you have established norms, you should review them before and after each meeting. Early childhood teams should all set their own norms. At the beginning of our principal team meetings in my school district, we would often decide on the norm that had been most difficult and focus on that one for our meeting. At the conclusion of the meeting, we would reflect on how well we had done. Remember, norms are a guide for behavior, and they should be posted and visible for all members to see.

In *Learning by Doing*, DuFour et al. (2016) offer six tips on creating norms:

1. Each team should create its own norms.
2. Norms should be stated as commitments to act or behave in certain ways rather than beliefs.
3. Norms should be reviewed at the beginning and end of each meeting for at least six months.
4. Teams should formally evaluate their effectiveness at least twice a year.
5. Teams should focus on a few essential norms rather than creating an extensive laundry list.
6. One of the team's norms should clarify how the team will respond if one or more are not observing the norms. (pp. 73–74)

Effective teams use outcome-driven agendas. Agendas are typically initiated by the team leader in a shared document, or team members can develop them at the end of a meeting for the next meeting. Agendas are specific to the work the teachers are focusing on. There cannot be a districtwide or a school team agenda because one size does not fit all. PreK teachers' agendas look different than elementary agendas, as their essential standards, targets, assessment, and data are unique to their age group. At Willow Grove, we used Google Docs to share our agendas. They were easily accessible for all staff. When shared before the meeting, an agenda provides all team members with clarity on the tasks they need to accomplish in the meeting. It is vital to have a clear agenda before the meeting so that members not only come prepared but also have had time to process important information. Shared agendas also give each team member the opportunity to add to the agenda items that they feel are important to discuss. Agendas should not include anything that can be shared in an email, memo, or announcement. They are about working on the four critical questions of a PLC. At the beginning of the meeting, it is useful to prioritize items and set time limits so that the team can cover topics in a timely fashion. The topics and key points from the discussion should also be shared after the meeting to notify other staff members of the meeting's outcomes. Many early childhood teams may find it difficult for all members to attend every meeting. Remember that it takes a lot of staff to implement quality programs for young children. As a principal who could not attend every team meeting, I found that the agenda made it easy to see what each team was working on, what it was struggling with, and how I could best support that team. Agendas are also useful if a team member is absent. Figure 3.6 provides a template you can use to create meeting agendas.

Meeting Agenda		
Meeting Agenda for: _____		
Meeting Date: _____ Time: _____ Place: _____		
Facilitator: _____		
Participants: _____		
Meeting Tasks		
Time Limit	Objective	Results

Source: Adapted from Marzano, Heflebower, Hoegh, Warrick, & Grift, 2016.

FIGURE 3.6: Meeting agenda template.

*Visit **go.SolutionTree.com/PLCbooks** for a free reproducible version of this figure.*

There are often specific roles team members can take, such as a recorder or note taker and usually a timekeeper. These members assist in organizing and focusing the meeting. The recorder or note taker enters an accurate record of decisions and discussions that occur during the meeting. He or she provides a formal account of who is at the meeting, what team members discuss, what actions they agree on, and who will carry out these actions. Having one recorder prevents other attendees from having to take their own notes and having their laptops open.

The timekeeper helps keep the meeting on schedule and reminds the members of time limits. This prevents running out of time at a meeting and not being able to address an important agenda item. Another role is what we would call the air traffic controller or process observer. His or her charge is to monitor participation levels and observe how the team members conduct their meeting (Mattos et al., 2016). It is sometimes best to rotate these positions so that everyone has a chance to fully participate.

Becoming a PLC translates into hard work. It is a powerful way of working together to achieve success for all students. It requires all teachers to focus on learning rather than teaching, work collaboratively on matters related to learning, and hold themselves accountable for the kind of results that fuel continual improvement.

Working on a collaborative team is neither optional nor invitational (Mattos et al., 2016). Teachers must commit to and contribute to the collaborative culture of the school by working on teams. Teams are the fundamental structure of a PLC. It is imperative that *all* teachers in a school participate on a team. When teachers are part of a team, they all have an equal stake in the learning that takes place in their school. Some schools no longer need whole-staff meetings, as the individual teams provide an efficient network of strong collaboration. Good, strong school teams "strengthen leadership, improve teaching and learning, nurture relationships, increase job satisfaction, and provide a means for mentoring and supporting new teachers and administrators" (Sparks, 2013, p. 28).

In the next chapter, we'll move on to the work that these teams tackle every day, starting with making sure that teachers are focusing on student learning rather than just their teaching, identifying essential standards, ensuring a guaranteed and viable curriculum, and addressing the first critical question.

Chapter 4

A Focus on Learning

Your brain has a capacity for learning that is virtually limitless, which makes every human a potential genius.

—*Michael J. Gelb*

In this chapter, I'll discuss in more detail the importance of student learning and how focusing on it may represent a fundamental shift in mindset. I'll explain how early childhood classroom configuration affects student learning in PLCs. I will also address the first critical question of a PLC: What do we want our students to know and be able to do? Answering this question means identifying essential standards and developing pacing for teaching them. I will explain how identifying these standards ensures a guaranteed and viable curriculum.

A Shift From Teaching Students to Students Learning

As we know, a school must focus on student learning. However, for years, many early childhood educators focused on teaching instead of learning. They taught skills during lessons, and that was that. They did the letter of the week and moved on to the next letter the following Monday. It was up to students to make sure that they learned what the teachers taught. The school might give teachers a state-directed, district-purchased, or required curriculum to follow—one program of study that supposedly covered everything they needed. Many were prepackaged and prescriptive, with numbered lessons, worksheets, planned activities, and assessment tools. Teachers used the plans, props, and books that went with each lesson and covered a certain amount of material over a specific time period. When I taught kindergarten (before Willow Grove) I had to be on a particular page of the district's scope and sequence every day of the school year. The scope and sequence document was a huge binder that I received on the day that I was hired;

it gave explicit instructions and directions on what to teach, when to teach, and how to teach. My job as a teacher was to dispense knowledge. Teaching, rather than learning, was the focus.

Research indicates that teachers dislike highly prescriptive programs, and this feeling can in turn diminish their long-term commitment to their work (Datnow & Castellano, 2000). Sadly, many prescriptive, packaged programs do not reflect a developmentally appropriate curriculum, which is crucial in any early childhood setting (Bredekamp & Copple, 1997). Many of the activities do not fit the students, and teachers tend to make their own adaptations to meet individual student needs. These types of programs also constrain teachers' creativity and autonomy.

Even if teachers did not receive a specific curriculum, they often relied on personal standbys, the things they loved for teaching—colors and shapes, the neighborhood, the farm, the seasons, dinosaurs, and so on. From these they developed their own curriculum. Lessons rooted in these types of curricula did no harm, but they did not necessarily support the learning that state and local standards hold teachers accountable for. As with the packaged programs, lessons like these come from a focus on teaching at the expense of a focus on learning.

To change this focus requires a shift in mindset. As I've discussed, a strong characteristic of effective PLCs is a clear and consistent focus on student learning. DuFour (2004) reiterates this notion when he writes that the mission "is not simply to ensure that students are taught but to ensure that they learn. This simple shift—from a focus on teaching to a focus on learning—has profound implications" (p. 8). Think about it: if you are not sure if a student has learned all the letters of the alphabet, how can you be sure that he or she will learn to read? Teachers need to ask themselves, "What standards does this dinosaur unit meet?" and "What will my students learn from this lesson?" It may be hard to give up those old standby units, but with so little time in a school day, every teacher must make the most of every minute. Sometimes teachers can still salvage old favorites by incorporating them into new lessons and linking them to essential standards. The bottom line is that everything teachers say and do must connect to essential learning.

Many studies have examined the relationship between teacher participation in PLCs and student achievement (Berry, Johnson, & Montgomery, 2005; Bolam, McMahon, Stoll, Thomas, & Wallace, 2005; Hollins, McIntyre, DeBose, Hollins, & Towner, 2004). They reveal that student learning improves when teachers work together in a PLC. Each of these studies reports student learning outcomes that indicate an intense focus on student learning; when educators participate in a PLC, teachers and students benefit, as demonstrated by improved achievement scores over time.

Further, Bolam et al. (2005) point out, "Pupil learning was the foremost concern of people working in PLCs and, the more developed a PLC appeared to be, the more positive was the association with two key measures of effectiveness—pupil achievement and professional learning" (p. 146).

Teachers who focus on their instructional practices often feel that they change the instructional culture of their schools: "Cultural change requires altering long-held assumptions, beliefs, expectations, and habits that represent the norm for people in the organization" (DuFour & Fullan, 2013, p. 2). I have found that it's possible to change opinions that students of poverty or those who speak another language will have difficulty learning at high levels. You can convince educators with those beliefs that these students can succeed. We all have those groups in our schools. And it does no good to deny that these kinds of excuses exist for their inability to learn.

PreK and preschool teachers are now responsible for preparing students for the K–12 school system. Often, they receive a set of standards for students to meet from their state or school district. Many states now have an overwhelming amount of early learning standards. As a teacher, there is not enough time in the day or the school year to teach all of them, let alone time for students to learn them. Sometimes district administrators will go through the state standards and then present them to the teachers. But teachers who receive standards from higher up in this way do not feel invested in them.

Where and how do these standards fit into daily class instruction? Some of the new curriculum series claim to have aligned their lessons with the standards. ABCmouse offers examples of activities that support the Common Core standards (ABCmouse.com, 2013). Creative Curriculum (http://teachingstrategies.com) offers a document that aligns Common Core standards with its own assessment system. These assurances may give teachers a false sense of confidence. It's easy to assume that if they are going along with the prescribed lessons, they will certainly teach all of the state standards. Yes, they are covering all of the standards, but the real question is, Are their students learning them? That is the most important question. Mattos et al. (2016) stress that a focus on learning "is a PLC's commitment to making student learning the fundamental purpose of the school or district" (p. 7). The ultimate goal of the PLC is to enhance student learning (Stoll, Bolam, McMahon, Wallace, & Thomas, 2006). In a review of the research, Vicki Vescio, Dorene Ross, and Alyson Adams (2008) find that student learning outcomes indicate that an intense focus on student learning and achievement is the aspect of learning communities that most impacts student learning.

Everything that you do, all practices, policies, and procedures, should focus on student learning. Nothing trumps learning. In their book *Learning by Doing*, DuFour et al. (2016) state that educators must make cultural shifts from focusing on teaching to focusing on learning, from emphasizing what was taught to a focus on what students learned, from coverage of content to demonstration of proficiency, and from providing teachers with state or district curricula to engaging collaborative teams to build shared knowledge regarding essential curricula. We need to consider preK classrooms part of the K–12 education system. We have the same responsibility for our students.

If it is the goal of schools to prepare students for higher-level learning, then there must be a schoolwide cultural shift from a focus on teaching to a focus on learning for each and every student as an individual: "The very essence of a *learning* community is a focus on and a commitment to the learning of each student" (DuFour et al., 2010, p. 11). This shift in focus involves every teacher at every age level and subject. PLCs foster a daily commitment to high levels of learning for *all*. This means that even our youngest students can learn at high levels, including students in preschool. They are each a part of the *all*. One way teachers of young children can ensure they include their students in the all is by maintaining a growth mindset. This goes for the teachers' beliefs about themselves and about students; they must believe that they themselves can learn new things and that their students can, too: "Students can and will do what educators believe they can do; if they put limits on students' abilities and potential, they essentially *guarantee* that those limits become learners' maximum potential" (Frizellie et al., 2016, p. 36).

The Configurations of Early Childhood Classrooms

If your school's mission statement focuses on student learning (as it should), then it includes every student in every program in your school from preschool on, including birth-to-three initiatives. Learning at high levels must mean that each student has learned the grade-level curriculum and has met the standards for that grade. Students in many preschool classrooms have disabilities, are not native English speakers, or are at risk for failure in school. They may be more challenging to teach, but they still require the opportunity to learn at high levels. The expectation for these students must be the same—that they will function independently after their school years, and to do this, they need the necessary knowledge and skills to be successful in college or careers.

The U.S. Department of Health and Human Services and the U.S. Department of Education (2015) released a policy statement that asserts, "All young children with disabilities should have access to inclusive high-quality early childhood programs, where they are provided with individualized and appropriate support in meeting high expectations" (p. 1). In other words, students deserve to participate in these programs no matter their ability. They benefit from learning together with same-aged peers and having extensive supports and services available in the least restrictive environment possible. All students in these classrooms develop a strong social-emotional foundation for future school engagement. This holds true for students at all grade levels (U.S. Department of Health and Human Services & U.S. Department of Education, 2015).

We must make every effort to reach this diversity of students in a general education preschool class, that is, a classroom that has typically developing students enrolled in it. The Common Core addresses the importance of meeting the learning needs of all students when it says, "Students with disabilities . . . must be challenged to excel within the general curriculum and be prepared for success in their post-school lives, including college and/or careers" (Ajayi & Collins-Parks, 2016, p. 15). Our schools must shift from assuming our standards are too rigorous for early childhood special education students, preschool students, or kindergarten students to expecting active engagement in learning them from all students. While we cannot modify standards for young children, we can include scaffolding, modifications, and accommodations in our instruction that are specific to each learner. As Heather Friziellie et al. (2016) note:

> We know that special education services are most effective when they:
>
> - Are delivered in the general education setting to the maximum extent possible
>
> - Are targeted to fill gaps between the student's disability and the demands of the setting
>
> - Ensure the same opportunities to achieve standards regardless of setting (p. 33)

When a teacher expects that a student will not be able to function independently as an adult, then he or she must adjust instruction.

Teachers of young children with autism or those with students who are severely disabled need to ask, "What do we want *this* student to know and be able to do?" This work may be hard for these educators, as they will need to develop a personalized curriculum for each student that aligns with IEP goals. The distance between the student's current reality and grade-level expectations may be vast, but the goal is still to work toward them (Friziellie et al., 2016). For this small percentage, collaborative teams that include the special education teacher and possibly the speech and language therapist, occupational therapist, social worker, and other members of the IEP team determine what a functional curriculum looks like. What will best prepare this student for his or her unique adult life? The team identifies goals that lead toward achievement and assesses them as it does for all students. They may be adapted to the student's needs, but they remain aligned to grade-level standards. The process and expectations remain the same. This student will learn at the highest levels possible. It is more important than ever when teaching students with disabilities to strive for a *growth mindset*—that is, the belief that improvement is possible with effort and support (Dweck, 2016). No matter the diversity of background or ability present in a class, the focus always stays in the same place: learning for all.

What Is a Guaranteed and Viable Curriculum?

When early childhood educators gather in their teams to collaborate and talk about student learning, what does this actually look like? What do they talk about? We know the discussions are not to determine what will be on the school supply list or how to arrange a field trip to the zoo, so what is it? The purpose of collaborative teams is to work together to build shared knowledge that, in turn, builds student learning. These powerful conversations will improve the quality and equity of student learning. They foster collective responsibility for *all* students' success. No longer is it acceptable to teach something simply because you always have, or because you think it is most important or like it the most.

Teachers' discussions should center on curriculum, assessment, and instruction grounded in evidence rather than opinion: "The fact that teachers collaborate will do nothing to improve a school. . . . The purpose of collaboration . . . can only be accomplished if the professionals engaged in collaboration *are focused on the right things*" (DuFour et al., 2006, p. 91). Conversations about how to focus collaboration begin by clarifying standards grade level by grade level, or age group by age group. What is it that we want all three-year-olds to know and be able to do? What is it that we want all preschool students, including students with IEPs, to know and be able to do before they enter kindergarten? What is it that we want all kindergarten students to know and be able to do so they are ready for first grade? What are the most important skills that they must learn to be successful at the next level? Early educators also need to align their curriculum standards to the grade levels above theirs: vertical progression. This ensures that there will be no gaps in a student's education. Educators will be able to see how the standards grow from grade level to grade level.

Very often, teachers feel every standard is important, and that they must teach each one with the same level of intensity. Not true. It is virtually impossible to teach and have your students learn every standard. There is simply not enough time in the school day or year. The key is to prioritize the standards rather than giving each one the same amount of attention. The best thing about prioritizing is that teachers can have great conversations focused on specific standards. They collaboratively gain clarity on what they want their students to learn. Isn't depth of a lesser number of key concepts and skills preferable to covering superficially every concept in the book? As W. James Popham (2003) writes:

> It is critical that all assessed standards be truly significant. From an instructional perspective, it is better for tests to measure a handful of powerful skills accurately than it is for tests to do an inaccurate job of measuring many skills. (p. 143)

It is vital to include kindergarten, early childhood, and special education educators in these conversations, and it is vital that kindergarten, early childhood, and special education educators participate in them. The students of these educators should also be held accountable for agreed-on standards, even special education students. Researchers point out, "The vast majority of special education students (80–85%) can meet the same achievement standards as other students if they are given specially designed instruction, appropriate access, supports, and accommodations, as required by IDEA [Individuals With Disabilities Education Act]" (Thurlow, Quenemoen, & Lazarus, 2016, p. 4).

According to Marzano (2003), the single and most important work that a school can do to raise student achievement is to determine and set a *guaranteed and viable curriculum*. This means we guarantee that all students, no matter who their teacher is, will receive adequate instruction on certain topics. This is the one factor that has the greatest impact on student achievement. Teachers still have flexibility in *how* to teach and meet the needs of each individual student, but there remains consistency in *what* they teach and in what students learn. You can still use the materials that the district or state require, or even favorite tried-and-true subjects like animals, colors, or dinosaurs, but the focus of the lessons is on the agreed-on targets. This is most important for special education teachers, as many of their students need scaffolding and modifications to be successful in achieving mastery of a standard or target. Teachers can do this by modeling and demonstrating particular skills. For example, when a student is building a block tower that keeps falling down, the teacher can build her own tower as a model and pose questions to help the student discover why hers doesn't fall. Teachers can break student learning into chunks or smaller pieces of learning, such as teaching a student to recognize a letter of the alphabet, then teaching the letter sound, and then finally teaching a word that begins with that sound.

A guaranteed curriculum ensures that every student receives the opportunity to learn the same core curriculum, which will equip them with the probability of success in school. Additionally, any student in a preschool program, no matter the location in the district, is guaranteed to be taught and learn the same thing. It is equally necessary that the guaranteed curriculum is *viable*. This means that enough time is available during the school day and year and that this time is protected, so that teachers will have the opportunity to teach the curriculum and their students will be able to learn it. There must be time within the school calendar for all content and skills to be taught and for students to learn (Marzano, 2003).

Teams collaboratively make decisions about what comprises a guaranteed and viable curriculum, and every teacher has the same responsibility to ensure that their students have learned what is most essential and significant. Making decisions together rather than individually may not be without sacrifice. You might have to throw out that old dinosaur unit that's always such a hit. Our favorite at Willow Grove centered on Johnny Appleseed. It was a difficult decision to let it go. The teachers loved it, the students loved it, and the parents loved it. They all looked forward to it. But the team determined that it did not cover enough essential standards that they were trying to teach, and therefore there wasn't enough time in the school calendar to include it.

Over the course of the school year, there needs to be enough time to teach the chosen essential standards to all students. That is what we are committed to— *all* students learning at high levels. The conversations that teacher teams have when determining essential standards for their students are invaluable. Yes, you can go to some websites and download standards for young children, but only you and your team members know *your* students. Teams must put in the work because it's only through these detailed collaborative conversations that they gain shared knowledge. Through this work, they can focus on best practices in teaching and learning.

As I previously stated, many early childhood educators are required to follow specific curricula such as Creative Curriculum, Head Start, and so on. While some are aligned to the standards in their states, many are not. The work of the collaborative team in a PLC focuses on the four critical questions, beginning with,

What do we want students to know and be able to do? (DuFour et al., 2016). The grade-level team's job is to determine the most important aspects of its identified curriculum. What are the priority items in Creative Curriculum, for example?

The team's conclusions should be a public document that it creates and shares with parents and families. This product states exactly what students are required to learn at each level of their education. Team members have agreed on what is most important. They are clear on what mastery looks like. They agree on specific items that will be taught and assessed. The focus is on what students *must know* to be proficient and not on what is *nice to know*. Basically, they agree to teach the same things in a common time frame. It is also important to vertically align the preschool document with those of the levels above and below. Preschool teachers should receive time to meet with birth-to-three programs, kindergarten teachers, and first-grade teachers to look at the alignment of their curricula. This is what vertical teams do.

The Need for Early Childhood Essential Standards

If you have received a curriculum to follow as an early childhood educator, you need time for your collaborative teams to identify the *essential standards* within the curriculum—the things that are most important for your students to learn. Many states now have early learning standards that outline what early childhood professionals can expect students between the ages of zero and five to know and be able to do in specific domains. Head Start programs are heavily regulated by the program performance standards. The Head Start Program Performance Standards (HSPPS) provide the foundation for all Head Start services: "The HSPPS reflect best practices and the latest research on early childhood development and brain science" (Office of Head Start, 2019).

Which of the standards should you prioritize? What specific targets lead to learning these standards? These are the standards that you must guarantee that *all* students know and that require common formative assessments. You will need to provide extra time and support to students who have not learned the standards. Conversely, if a student already knows them, you will provide an extension for that student.

You can try to teach every standard, but will your students learn them all? I don't think so. There are far too many at each level, and that is why collaborative teams must decide on those that are most important. Schools cannot leave it up to each individual teacher to decide what is most important. It must be the decision of the team. The first year that I was a principal in a school with fifteen kindergarten classrooms, I was stunned when report cards came out. Each teacher based their reporting on what they thought was most important. Fifteen different perspectives! What a different education each student was getting. This was most apparent during the following school year, when these students were split up among four schools for first grade. Each first-grade teacher had a smattering of students from fifteen different kindergarten teachers, and those students had learned what was most important to their teacher. Some students, for example, were counting to one hundred by fives, while others were only counting to one hundred by ones. Now it was up to the first-grade teacher to even things out. Talk about not providing equity.

Mike Schmoker (2011) believes that teams must reduce the content standards by 50 percent. In doing so, teachers will have fewer standards but will be able to teach the ones that they focus on with adequate depth, meaning all students will learn and retain more. This does not mean that every standard is not taught. This means that teams must prioritize standards and determine what is most important, because all standards are not equal in value. When my teachers were discussing what was most important for a four-year-old to learn, there were many lively conversations. What shapes were most important? What colors were a must to learn? Each team member has the right and the duty to be heard. Every team member must be a part of the group dialogue. In the book *Rigorous Curriculum Design*, essential standards are defined as:

> a carefully selected subset of the total list of grade specific standards within each content area that students must know and be able to do by the end of each school year in order to be prepared to enter the next grade. (Ainsworth, 2010, p. 39–40)

I discuss the specific process that early childhood educators can use to determine essential standards in the following sections.

What Do We Want Our Students to Know and Be Able to Do?

So far, I've talked a lot about how important essential standards are and how teams must work together to identify them. So, how do you actually do it? What is the process for determining the essential standards for our youngest learners? How long does this take, and where do you start? Remember, this is a process and not an activity. Going through standards and considering which are most important takes time, as well as much conversation and collaboration. You should commit to starting with one subject area at a time, and don't be alarmed if it takes a good part of the school year. Remember, the work of a PLC is an ongoing process.

The first consideration is whether you have a state-designated set of early learner standards, a set of curriculum standards, or district learner standards. Teachers can draw from these sources, using individual standards and targets from these standards to determine what is most important and to prioritize and pace. Standards from Creative Curriculum, State Early Childhood Standards, Opening the World of Learning (OWL), or the Common Core kindergarten standards (NGA & CCSSO, 2010a, 2010b) are a few of the many documents that can be used as starting points to determine what is most important for *all* preschool students to know and be able to do to be prepared for kindergarten. I say starting points because each of these sources contains far more standards than you can teach or than students can learn in one school year. It is an impossible task, so you must narrow the list down to what is most essential. The task is to identify the essential standards at your grade or age level. Teacher teams must carefully select and agree on what is most essential.

Reeves (2002) suggests that there are three major filters one can use to determine what makes a standard essential. The first is *endurance*. A standard that has endurance is one that represents learning that goes beyond a specific grade level and that students will need to know for a longer period of time. The following description of enduring standards is an apt one: "These are standards that are used during subsequent units of instruction and over a period of years" (Bailey & Jakicic, 2012, p. 30). An enduring standard represents a skill or concept that is important in life. You can ask, "Do students need to know this for the long haul?" *Endurance* means that the student will use this skill year after year. For example, young children need to learn the beginning principles of writing. The following standard from the Illinois Early Learning and Development Standards for Preschool would satisfy this need, and thus we would call it an essential standard: "Use scribbles, letterlike forms, or letters/words to represent written language" (5.A.ECb; Illinois State Board of Education, 2013).

Preschoolers who pretend to write are showing that they know that print has meaning. Drawing and scribbling are the first steps in using the skills they will need later for writing. Although it may not make sense to adults, scribbling is very important to a young child. Usually, they can tell you what their scribbles mean, and there is a purpose to their writing.

The second filter to use when determining an essential standard is *readiness*. Is this skill necessary for the next level of learning? What skills are necessary for kindergarten or first grade? The standard should contain prerequisite content or skills that are required for the next unit, course, or grade level. Here is an example from the Common Core English language arts: "Demonstrate basic knowledge of one-to-one letter-sound correspondences by producing the primary sound or many of the most frequent sounds for each consonant" (RF.K.3a; NGA & CCSSO, 2010a).

Learning about letters is an important foundation for literacy development. Knowledge about the predictable relationships between sounds and letters allows students to apply these relationships to both familiar and unfamiliar words, and to begin to read fluently. Efficient and automatic sound-symbol correspondence leads to accurate phonetic analysis and is a vital aspect of the process of learning to read.

The third filter is *leverage*. This is learning that is applied within a variety of content areas. It is important that students learn skills that they will use in different disciplines throughout their school, career, and life situations. Kim Bailey and Chris Jakicic (2012) call this a "'bang for your buck' standard" (p. 31). Some states have the same standards in two different curricular areas. An example would be that students are taught how to read a graph in mathematics, but they can also use this skill in science. Students will be expected to apply these skills in multiple or future academic areas. The Illinois Early Learning and Development Standards for Preschool identify one of these classical applicable skills with the following: "Organize, represent, and analyze information using concrete objects, pictures, and graphs, with teacher support" (10.B.ECa; Illinois State Board of Education, 2013). Graphing is an important mathematics tool. It is also a skill that introduces broader concepts, such as greater than and less than, most and least, and so on. Preschool classrooms often use bar graphs of how many students have their birthday in each month. Introducing graphs at an early age can help students understand mathematical and scientific concepts such as sorting, organizing, counting, comparing, and analyzing. Gathering, collecting, and interpreting numerical information is increasingly necessary in a world that is inundated by data.

A Protocol for Determining Essential Standards

Before the actual work of determining essential standards begins, the stage must be set. Each team member should have access to standards that he or she is currently using, standards that are required, or standards that they would like to incorporate into their curriculum. Prior to the meeting, teachers should individually familiarize themselves with the standards that they will use for the process.

Unlike teachers in the elementary grades, early childhood teachers often have a variety of resources to use when determining essential standards for preschoolers. Some useful materials could be the CCSS for kindergarten, your state's early learning standards, Head Start performance standards, Teaching Strategies' (n.d.) Creative Curriculum objectives, and so on. Your district may already have a set of standards that you are required to use, and those should be handy too. It is also helpful to have standards for before and after your grade level. For example, kindergarten teams should have copies of first-grade standards as well as preschool standards, if available. It is very helpful for each member of the team to understand the full process that will be used to determine essential standards. I break it down into five steps.

Step One

I recommend completing one subject area at a time. It may take a school year to cover the standards in one subject area. At Willow Grove, we began with mathematics and then moved on to language arts the following year. The team should discuss and review the terms *endurance, readiness,* and *leverage* (Ainsworth, 2004). It is important that there is a clear understanding of these three major filters, as they will help you determine which standards are essential.

Step Two

After determining what set of standards to use, team members independently highlight those individual standards they feel to be essential, keeping in mind the need for endurance, readiness, and leverage (Ainsworth, 2004). By giving teachers about twenty minutes to do this at the beginning of the meeting, you can be assured that everyone has taken about the same amount of time and has not overthought each standard. If you spend too much time on this part of the process, you may end up highlighting every standard! The result should be a variety of standards, as teachers' total selections will not be the same ones. On the other hand, teachers will choose some of the same or similar standards, which certainly tells you something about teacher recognition of the value of certain standards.

Step Three

It is during this step that team members come to agreement on what they believe to be essential. This collaborative process removes issues with individual choice; often those decisions are based on a teacher's comfort level, availability of resources, or personal preferences. If teachers choose independently, then all students do not have access to a guaranteed and viable curriculum.

Some teams begin step three by listing the standards that every individual highlighted. There is probably no need to discuss these at great length, as all teachers already agree on their importance. They then exclude standards that everyone agrees are not essential (that is, those that no one highlighted). Lastly, the team goes through the remaining standards. This is where the fun begins, and where teachers gain clarity on each standard. They discuss what it looks like when a student has mastered a specific skill. Teachers explain their reasoning for why they believe something is essential. There may be conversations on determining, for example, what colors or shapes students need to be able to identify by the time they are five years old. During this time, everyone should have a voice and be heard, because there must be agreement on the outcome. This step builds team consensus on which standards are essential (Ainsworth, 2004). This part of the process may be lengthy and may take up to an hour.

Step Four

In this step, the team determines alignment between its draft of essential standards and any other related documentation they may have (Bailey & Jakicic, 2017). In the upper grades, essential standards can be compared to the state standards and what the state test emphasizes. It's ideal for preschool teachers to align their instruction to a developmental continuum document, such as *A Developmental Continuum From Early Infancy to Kindergarten Entry* developed by the California Department of Education (2015). It is a formative assessment instrument for young children that is used to inform instruction and program development. It measures progress and mastery toward desired outcomes (essential standards).

It is important that the essential standards the team chooses reflect the assessment you use. In other words, the standards that you determine essential are ones that you assess on the test. That connection must be there. If you are going to teach it, and you want your students to learn it, then you need to assess it. You are not teaching to the test but instead making sure that the end goal is clear. Teams may do some revisions at this point, as the version they have so far is only a draft. This step is shorter in length and may only take fifteen to twenty minutes.

Step Five

This is the time to review alignment vertically. It is best for the grade-level team that has been doing the work to review vertical alignment, but it is always beneficial to have the vertical teams take a look to ensure alignment and no gaps. Preschool teachers can look at birth-to-three standards and kindergarten standards. They should be searching for any gaps or redundancies. If there is a standard for preschoolers to be able to count from one to ten, for example, then this skill should not be a standard for kindergarten students. Students should learn it before kindergarten. If a student enters kindergarten without this skill in place, then he or she should receive extra time and support to achieve it. They would also check to see that certain areas are highly represented, such as phonemic awareness, an essential skill that lays the foundation for reading. If it's not, team members now know to address that gap.

Standards should not be identical at each grade level, although they may be more rigorous at higher grade levels or age groups. Counting standards become more rigorous as students get older. In preschool, for example, the general expectation is for students to count from one to five, in kindergarten the expectation is to count from one to one hundred, and by first grade, students should be able to count to one hundred and twenty starting at any number. Many times, vertical team members meet in person to discuss their thoughts and to determine learning progressions. Popham (2007) defines a learning progression as a "sequenced set of building blocks that students must master en route to mastering a more distant curricular aim" (p. 83). The teams consider their expectations for proficiency at each level.

Collaborative teams have studied the intended, assigned, or given curriculum together. They have sorted through all the standards and reached consensus on what is essential—what is really important. They have discussed and agreed on what mastery looks like for their students. They have determined what specific knowledge and skills look like for each target. They now have a document of essential standards that each team member agrees on. There is clarity and consensus on each skill. It is also vertically aligned with other teams or grade levels in the district. Lastly, they pledge to one another that they will in fact teach the agreed-on curriculum (DuFour & DuFour, 2012). It all sounds like a pretty simple process, doesn't it? Well, it doesn't have to be perfect at the onset, or ever, for that matter. Standards can be a living, breathing document that you reassess every year. At the beginning, or the end, of each school year, you can make adjustments, such as adding, deleting, or clarifying items. When we did this at my school, we still had a huge, unmanageable list of standards, many more than we could ever teach or have the students learn. This was difficult to accept because we had discussed all of them and felt that we had compiled the most essential standards. We could teach them all in the school year, but the students could not have learned them all. We realized that with so many standards, we couldn't ensure that we would teach them all effectively. So it was back to the drawing board. As the year progressed, we made changes and deletions and eventually came up with a much more manageable list.

Figure 4.1 is an example of the essential standards in mathematics for early childhood students at Willow Grove. It specifies what they want their students to know and be able to do to be ready for kindergarten. They have aligned their standards vertically to flow easily into the kindergarten mathematics standards.

Early Childhood Mathematics 2018–2019

Goal 6					
4.0 Expectation	3.0 Target	2.0 Expectation	T1	T2	T3
See Rubric	6.A.ECf: Verbally recite numbers from 1 to 10.	See Rubric	X	X	X
See Rubric	6.B.ECb: Show understanding of how to count out and construct sets of objects of a given number up to 5.	See Rubric	X	X	X
See Rubric	6.D.ECb: Describe comparisons with appropriate vocabulary, such as "more," "less," "greater than," "fewer," "equal to," or "same as."	See Rubric	X	X	X
Goal 8					
4.0 Expectation	3.0 Target	2.0 Expectation	T1	T2	T3
See Rubric	8.A.ECa: Sort, order, compare, and describe objects according to characteristics or attributes.		X	X	X
Goal 9					
4.0 Expectation	3.0 Target	2.0 Expectation	T1	T2	T3
N/A	9.B.ECb: Use appropriate vocabulary for identifying locations and ordinal position.		X	X	X

Source for standards: Illinois State Board of Education, 2013.
Source: ©2018 by Kildeer Countryside CCSD 96. Adapted with permission.

FIGURE 4.1: Sample early childhood essential mathematics standards.

How to Pace the Standards

Once teams have followed the protocol for determining essential standards, the next step is to develop a common pacing guide (refer to chapter 3, pages 56–62, for examples). Pacing guides go under many different names—*scope and sequence, curriculum map,* or *instructional calendar.* This guide is an educator's road map for the school year. It is the sequence of instruction that all team members follow. These guides ensure that each teacher has adequate time to teach specific targets, assess student learning, and provide corrective instruction.

Generally, it is best to develop a yearlong pacing guide to ensure that you include and teach all the essential standards. When using this type of pacing guide, teachers determine beforehand when they will teach targets, when they will assess them, and when interventions will take place. It's best for all teachers to conduct assessment of student learning on the same day so that no class has more or fewer learning days. By specifying an assessment date, all teachers can have their data recorded in time for the team discussion.

If preschool classrooms are scattered across a district, a pacing guide provides equity for all the young learners in the district. It is generally a series of cycles: teach, assess, look at data, reteach if necessary, assess, look at data again, and intervene. Many schools use weekly pacing guides as opposed to daily guides because it can be difficult for teachers to teach the exact same thing on a certain day at a certain time. They are more like a sequence of instruction than a daily prescription to be followed. There may be targets that take longer for students to learn, and teams should consider this when developing the guide. The targets in a preschool setting usually span several years, meaning that by the time a student completes the preschool program and is ready to move on to kindergarten, he or she should have learned the essential standards. Some students may learn to count from one to five when they are three years old, and some may not achieve this until they are four. It just depends on where they are developmentally. As educators of young children, we know that early learning develops at varying rates. When determining a pacing guide, teachers must consider the individual developmental paths that students follow. That is why the following question should be asked: "What is it we want our students to know and be able to do before they enter kindergarten?" By doing this, teachers can use the guide with an eye toward moving all students forward in all areas. This allows each teacher to instruct his or her students based on the needs of the individual students in the class. As you go through the school year, it is important to discuss and note how the pacing guide is working. By doing this, you can keep a record of any necessary adjustments to make for the following school year. Many times, team members may determine that some targets take more or less time than they thought they would, and the team can adjust the pacing for successful learning.

Early childhood teachers now have documents describing what their preschool students will be learning and when they will be learning. They know when they will be assessing student skills and when they will meet as a team to discuss their results. The agreed-on standards and pacing guide can be extremely useful to any new teacher in the program as well as to parents. It is important to share these documents with students' families, so they too know what their children are learning. With this important foundation in place, we can now move on to discussing in more detail how assessment works in an early childhood setting.

Chapter 5

Assessment

*Assessment is today's means of modifying
tomorrow's instruction.*

—Carol Ann Tomlinson

In this chapter, we will look at the second of the four critical questions of a PLC (How will we know if they have learned it? [DuFour et al., 2016]). The way to find out is to assess students' learning. Assessment can be a touchy subject for early childhood educators. Many feel strongly that most types of early childhood assessments are not developmentally appropriate. Testing is often frowned on in early childhood circles, and I was no exception.

When I became a principal in 1999, my superintendent asked me, "What would cause you to put your keys on the table?" In other words, what would cause me to resign? For me the answer was easy. If I had to make my teachers test young children, then I would be out the door. I felt that the testing of young children was just not appropriate. Testing, as I understood it at the time, was reading questions and filling in the bubbles on an answer sheet. What three-, four-, or five-year-old could do that—or should do that?

When my son was in kindergarten (way back in the 1990s), he came home from school crying and reported that he didn't want to go anymore. When I asked him why, he told me that his arm was tired of "filling in all those circles on the paper." I immediately called the teacher and brought up the issue. She laughed and said that they were giving the Metropolitan Reading Readiness Test to the students and would continue it for the next three days. I responded that my son would not be in school for the next three days. She was shocked. How was she going to know what my son knew if he didn't take the test?

As a kindergarten teacher myself, I knew that there were other appropriate ways to determine this and told her I would be glad to share this with her if she had the time. Unfortunately, she never did seek my input. I wanted to point out to her that she could use observation instead of standardized testing. I could have told her that it's easy to know if a student has learned to recognize the letters of the alphabet through games, checklists, or even photographs. I suspect, however, that her administrator mandated the test and she was unwilling to push back. I did keep my son home for the rest of the test. After the testing period, he returned to school and, believe it or not, he did learn to read.

Standardized tests can put enormous pressure on a young learner. Researcher Laura Nicholson (2016) explains that they can make a student feel anxious, incompetent, or even bored. These psychological symptoms can even combine with physiological problems (tight muscles, trembling; Nicholson, 2016). Standardized assessments, where examiners strictly follow instructions for test administration, pose dangers in restricting the expression of diversity, and undervaluing students' individual needs and learning styles in early childhood settings (Gullo, 2006). Dominic F. Gullo and Kim Hughes (2011) assert that assessment should be integrated into teaching. Teachers need to teach while finding opportunities to document learning. Doing this makes students feel more comfortable, and that assessment is just part of the teaching and learning process.

Under the Every Student Succeeds Act (ESSA, 2015), states must administer annual statewide tests in reading or language arts and mathematics to all students in grades 3 through 8. These are standardized tests that provide annual measures of student progress. Remember the story about my son in kindergarten? That was a standardized test. His experience is why I really believe that he has always felt that he "doesn't do well" on tests. But early childhood programs receiving federal and state funding generally require assessment as an accountability measure. These assessments can be seen as a return on investment in improving school readiness for young children. On December 2, 2007, President Bush signed the Improving Head Start for School Readiness Act, which included provisions to strengthen Head Start quality: program monitoring, the review of childhood outcomes, and financial auditing (Office of Head Start, 2019). This type of testing is not formative assessment. The purpose is not to guide student instruction but to measure knowledge. In PLCs, remember, the purpose of an assessment is to monitor student learning and identify students who need more time and support.

Years later my new superintendent asked me the same question: "What would cause you to put your keys on the table?" Strangely enough, my response had changed completely. If I was told to stop assessing young children, then I would turn in my keys. My whole attitude on the assessment of young children has changed dramatically. I was now tuned into appropriate assessment of our youngest learners and collecting data to improve instruction.

Documenting what young children have learned can be challenging, but I now believe this is the only way that a teacher can be assured that the student has mastered a target and learned the skills that the teams have identified as necessary. I now very much agree with the following statement: "The early years of schooling, prekindergarten through third grade, is the time to begin the processing of assessing children's performance related to the standards" (Helm & Gronlund, 1999).

Why Assess Early Childhood Students?

In an article in *Early Childhood News*, Susan Bowers (2008) states that the primary reasons for assessment are to screen for disabilities; to assess kindergarten readiness; to assist in developing curriculum and daily activities; to evaluate the effectiveness of a project or a program; and to provide feedback to parents. As researchers and practitioners learn more about how early childhood assessment can and should be used, the reasons for conducting early childhood assessments shift from accountability efforts to a focus on ways to improve instructional practices and to determine a student's mastery of specific skills. This calls for a shift in teacher mindset as well: "Assessment should not be considered an end point—something you do to prepare a report for families or to meet a program's requirements" (Jablon, Dombrow, & Dichtelmiller, 1999, p. 1). Instead, think of assessment as part of a learning cycle (Bailey & Jakicic, 2012).

The assessment cycle in early childhood begins when the team creates an essential standards document and a pacing guide, which we covered in the previous chapter (page 84). Classroom teachers then use this pacing guide to plan instruction for large groups, small groups, and individual students.

Effective teachers choose strategies that fit their classroom situation and dynamics. They can get a sense of this by considering what the students already know and can do. Generally, teachers can administer a preassessment to determine this. Then they deliver differentiated instruction, using whatever strategies will work best for the learning needs they have identified. The next step is to assess (which may take the form of observations, checklists, anecdotal notes, video, work samples, and so on). Whatever form they take, teacher teams created them. After compiling the data, teachers meet to discuss the data and determine evidence of learning and the need for additional instruction (I further explore data team meetings in chapter 6, page 103). Teachers share their data with one another, and conversations revolve around how to respond. This process is ongoing and continual, as shown in figure 5.1 (page 90). Teachers then move on to the next standard to be taught and assessed.

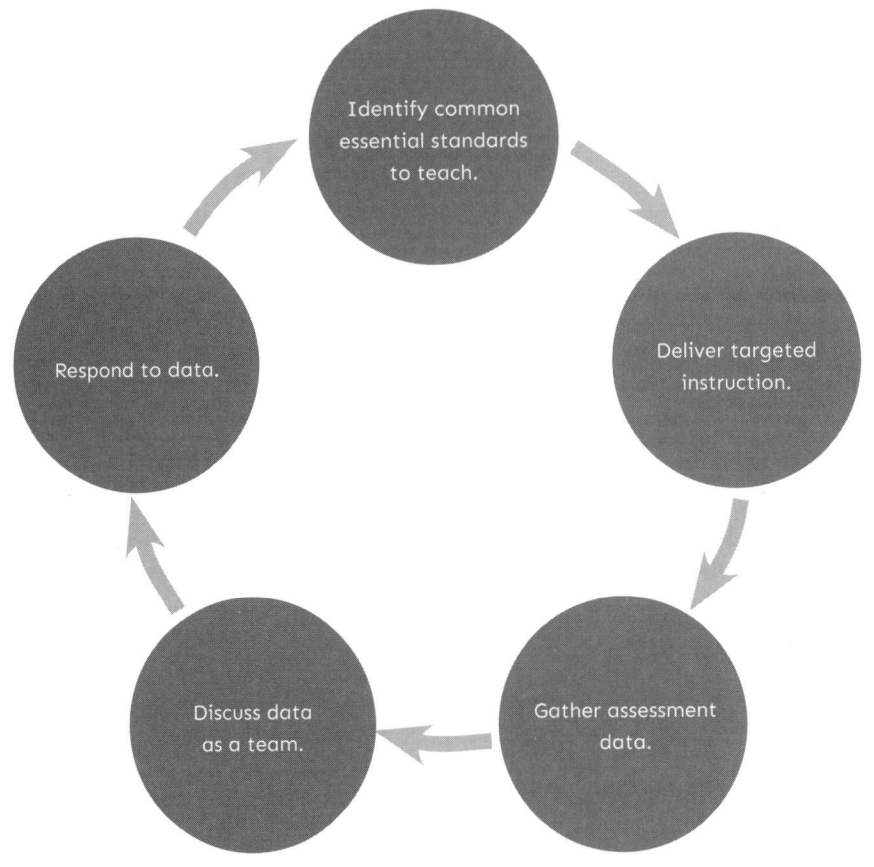

FIGURE 5.1: The early childhood assessment cycle.

Early childhood assessment is intended to be an ongoing process whereby adults who are familiar with the student gather data (for example, observations, video, work samples, and so on) about the student in his or her natural environment and while he or she is participating in natural routines. Assessment should be embedded into the daily classroom routine. For teachers of young children this type of formative assessment is ongoing. It is informing their instruction. Teachers of young children know they are continually assessing their students as they get immediate feedback when checking for understanding with questions; monitoring students as they work independently and in groups; and using exit slips, clickers, and whiteboards (Bailey & Jakicic, 2012). Teachers collect and document information, reflect on it, and use that information to support their students. This type of assessment has been labeled as *authentic assessment* (Bagnato & Yeh-Ho, 2006; Morrison, 2017).

The assessment of young children should be the driving force behind the classroom teacher's instruction. In PLCs, *common formative assessments* are designed to gather information in order to make informed instructional decisions. This type of assessment is "typically created collaboratively by a team of teachers responsible for the same grade level or course" (AllThingsPLC, 2016). Using ongoing assessment information to guide instructional decisions is the primary purpose of early childhood assessment and should be a component of every high-quality early childhood program (National Association for the Education of Young Children & National Association of Early Childhood Specialists in State Departments of Education [NAEYC & NAECS/SDE], 2003). Documentation of a student's performance provides evidence of their learning. Teachers document factual observations and link them to essential standards. Linking their assessment to essential standards is critical. Every standard should have an assessment connected to it. By doing this, teachers will know if students have mastered a target and are ready to move forward in their learning.

In PLCs, educators actively seek desired results. They want and need evidence that their students have learned what they've taught. If you have proof that a student has not learned to recognize the letters of the alphabet, then it is your moral obligation to go back and make sure that he or she can recognize them. You can't just hope that a student can recognize the letters of the alphabet. That is not good enough. How will they ever be able to read if they don't know their letters?

Assessment informs and drives instruction: "Assessment is the process of gathering evidence of student learning to inform educational decisions" (Stiggins, 2017, p. 5). Richard J. Stiggins (1985) also finds that information teachers use and need most to teach individual students does not come from standardized tests. Thomas Guskey (2003) believes that the assessments teachers administer on a regular basis in their classrooms are the ones that guide improvements in their teaching. Instead, teachers rely on information that they gather from tests they make themselves or from structured performance samples. Good assessments assist teachers in making critical decisions about curriculum, classroom materials, and personal interactions. It is an integral part of a process that reviews information about a student and then uses that information to plan educational activities that are at a level the student can understand and is able to learn from. It informs instruction. Why would you teach something that a student already knows?

At Willow Grove, the first assessment we took data on was letter recognition. Teachers were pleasantly surprised when the results showed that almost 92 percent of the students had already met that target. Staff learned that letter recognition would be the focus for a few of their students, but not all, and they knew exactly who those students were. That was when we threw the "letter-of-the-week" program out the door!

What Do Preschool and Kindergarten Assessments Look Like?

The methods schools use to assess young children can be very different from the methods schools use for school-aged students. There are basically two different types of assessment systems: (1) those that teacher teams develop and (2) those that are purchased.

Teacher Team–Created Assessments

Assessment systems that teacher teams develop themselves can easily align to a program's philosophy and curriculum. They can be directly connected to essential standards—the things that you want your students to know and be able to do.

As an early childhood teacher, you observe students all the time in everyday, authentic experiences. The best assessment process in early childhood is systematic, ongoing, observational assessment. Assessment should be the act of seeing and looking at students. It is to look at a student, to see where the student is, to see what the student can do, and finally to see what the student needs assistance with or what he or she cannot do. It takes into consideration students' capabilities, needs, and interests, and uses observation as the main tool for gathering data. It should make sense for the students and benefit them. Beyond just seeing, teachers can build on and extend where the student is, using this knowledge as a basis for their planning and decision making, and adapting their practice to the information they gather.

Teachers should create assessments for preschool and kindergarten students through the work of the collaborative team. The assessment system should incorporate simple, easy-to-use tools and templates to make the process more manageable for educators. It is no longer up to individual teachers to determine if a student has mastered a target or standard. Remember, the team has agreed on what is essential, so the team needs to agree on what that looks like for their students. Assessments should be aligned to the targets and pacing the team agreed on. Targets and pacing are very necessary to determine progress on IEP goals.

Teacher teams should design assessments for young children that use developmentally appropriate practices, such as informal observations and performance assessments. These types of assessment are more in line with the developmental characteristics of young children. Many can be administered in conjunction with instruction. The National Association for the Education of Young

Children (NAEYC) and the National Association of Early Childhood Specialists in State Departments of Education (NAECS/SDE; 2003) assert:

> To assess young children's strengths, progress, and needs, use assessment methods that are developmentally appropriate, culturally and linguistically responsive, tied to children's daily activities, supported by professional development, inclusive of families, and connected to specific, beneficial purposes: (1) making sound decisions about teaching and learning, (2) identifying significant concerns that may require focused intervention for individual children, and (3) helping programs improve their educational and developmental interventions. (p. 1)

Observational methods of assessment are the primary technique that early childhood educators choose when assessing their students. Many teachers identify high-quality observation as the most important authentic assessment by which they collect data. *Observation* is the practice of collecting information by watching and listening to students with the intent to use the information gleaned from the observation to enrich student learning. Observations should be open and unobtrusive, whether using an observational checklist, anecdotal record, language sample, work sample, or a performance evaluation. Teachers should conduct them in a variety of settings to avoid wrongly overgeneralizing. They can focus their observations in many different ways: conducting them in a specific area of the classroom or on a determined activity; concentrating on one student or on a small group of students; focusing on a domain or area of learning (such as fine motor skills or mathematics); or zeroing in on a specific standard or target (such as recognition of shapes).

When observing, teachers should document only the facts—what they see and hear. They should not make interpretations, but they should use their professional judgment in order to get a representative picture of what the student has learned. Teachers of young children know that a student knows one thing one day and doesn't know it the next. If a student demonstrates the ability to identify his or her name more often than not, the teacher should make an informed decision based on knowledge of that particular child.

According to Bailey and Jakicic (2012), authentic assessments or performance assessments demonstrate proficiency on a skill. It requires students to apply what they have learned to a new situation. Teachers can assess gross motor skills this way as well as students' ability to write their names. There are a variety of ways to collect documentation in classrooms for the young learner. These ways include checklists, anecdotal notes, and rubrics.

Checklists

It is imperative that all classroom teachers conduct and record these types of observational assessments in a similar fashion across all preschool students in a school or district. This provides equity among programs and classrooms. One way to achieve this is for teachers to record their observations on a checklist that the teacher team creates. A checklist identifies what the observer is going to look at when observing the student, naming specific behaviors and skills in a logical order and, at times, even defining specific language that the assessor should use when interacting with the student during the assessment. Checklists are predetermined, clear, and specific lists that identify knowledge, skills, or aptitudes. Teachers can track planned activities that each student has completed using a checklist. When collaborative teams develop observational checklists, they spend time discussing what mastery of each specific target looks like and they agree on proficiency.

Teams can put skills like counting objects, identifying shapes, and many others into checklist format. The teacher can observe this skill during play or even set up an activity for students to engage in. The number recognition assessment in figure 5.2 states clear directions and exactly what the assessor should say. This clarity ensures that the information teachers gather is equitable for all students. Preschool teachers can use this tool when providing small-group instruction for their students.

Number Recognition

Directions: Ask the student to identify these numbers that are in random order. Say: "Can you point to each number and say its name for me?"

9	4	12	17	10	6	14	2	8	16
13	7	3	18	1	15	19	5	11	20

FIGURE 5.2: Sample number recognition assessment.

If a teacher wants to observe gross motor skill development, he or she can lay out an obstacle course and use a developmental checklist to record the skills of all of the students as they play on the balance beam, climb stairs, or bend and crawl under a board.

At Willow Grove, kindergarten students had over fifty sight words to learn by the end of the school year. Teachers would tape groups of sight words at the classroom entrance. As students entered the classroom, the aide had them point at and say the words. She had a simple checklist and could assess this target several times during the course of the week. The team had decided previously that a student has mastered each word after five correct identifications. Figure 5.3 offers an easy way to check for sight word recognition. The assessor makes a checkmark next to the word each time the student identifies it correctly.

Sight Words					
Student name:					
Unit 1		Unit 2		Unit 3	
Word	Correct	Word	Correct	Word	Correct
I		have		me	
am		is		with	
the		we		she	
little		like		see	
a		my		look	
to		he		they	
**can		for		you	
**play		**want		of	
		**make		**will	
				**and	

**Bonus Words

FIGURE 5.3: Sight word checklist.

Figure 5.4 (page 96) provides a template you can use to create your own sight word checklists.

Anecdotal Notes

Another way a teacher can record and organize observations is by taking anecdotal notes, keeping a pad of paper and pencil in his or her pocket and using them to write down phrases or describe key events in an interaction. Keeping scrap paper and pencils around the room is another way to have the tools available for documenting meaningful anecdotal information. I always kept sticky notes nearby to scribble down an observation. By the end of the day, my desk was covered with them. These days, you might keep your smartphone or classroom tablet with you to record your notes in a note-taking app. I have had students ask what I am doing, and I always let them know that I was writing down the wonderful

Sight Word Checklist		
Unit: _____	Unit: _____	Unit: _____

FIGURE 5.4: Sight word checklist template.

Visit ***go.SolutionTree.com/PLCbooks*** *for a free reproducible version of this figure.*

things that they had learned. At the end of the day, you can record your notes onto a checklist, rubric, or other organizer, and share them at a future team data meeting. You can also post the information to an electronic team data wall, which is an online document that teacher teams can share. Team members can manipulate them and view pertinent information on their students. They can be great to aggregate and organize student data. At Willow Grove we used Google Docs.

Assessment

Figures 5.5 and 5.6 (page 98) are examples of different ways that a teacher can collect data. Figure 5.5 is a simple recording sheet to keep notes on a student and a skill that he or she is working on or has mastered. Figure 5.6 is to help record information for a specific target the teacher is observing in a small-group setting.

Observation Recording Sheet

Student's Name	Date and Activity
Paul J.	3/30 Playing with cars, counted five of them. One-to-one correspondence.
Mary S.	3/30 Unable to count cars while playing with another student. No one-to-one.
Layla F.	3/30 No counting skills.
Mark M.	3/30 Counting cars to 10. One-to-one correspondence.

FIGURE 5.5: Observation recording sheet.

*Visit **go.SolutionTree.com/PLCbooks** for a free reproducible version of this figure.*

Small-Group Observation Form	
Date: 3/30	Activity: Counting toy cars
Target: Show understanding of how to count out and construct sets of objects of a given number up to 5. (6.B.ECb; Illinois State Board of Education, 2013).	
Student's Name: Paul J. Counted toy cars 1–5	Student's Name: Mary S. Unable to count cars
Student's Name: Layla F. Unable to count cars	Student's Name: Mark M. Counted 10 cars!
Student's Name:	Student's Name:
Student's Name:	Student's Name:

FIGURE 5.6: Small-group observation form.

Visit **go.SolutionTree.com/PLCbooks** *for a free reproducible version of this figure.*

Rubrics

A rubric is another assessment tool that is useful for certain purposes. The main function is performance assessment. For some performances, a teacher will observe a student in the process of doing something, such as riding a tricycle, walking on a balance beam, and so on. For other performances, the teacher reviews the work that the student produced, such as artwork, writing, and projects. Sometimes it's best to use photos or audiovisual recordings to help capture student performances. Teachers can take videos of students doing a somersault or hopping on one foot, for example. The PE teacher can video his or her whole class jumping on one foot and later review the video to note which students had achieved the target. Photos of student work (such as their written names) taken by the teacher can show that a student has acquired a skill. Work samples are an excellent way to capture what a student knows and can do and what he or she doesn't know and can't do.

In general, a *rubric* is a set of criteria for student work that includes descriptions of levels of performance quality. Rubrics that are designed by teachers are a good way to evaluate the performance of students because of the way they can break down the quality of the student work. Each level of performance quality can list specific criteria for scoring the quality of student work or performance. A checklist can note the number of shapes or the actual shapes that a student can identify, but a rubric can include the level of learning that each student exhibits by assigning each level to a corresponding description.

Teachers can use rubrics for many things, including for assessing preschool writing. I once had a discussion with a group of teachers on what mastery looked like when a student wrote his or her name. One teacher felt that if she could read it, it was mastered. Another teacher felt that mastery required capital letters, lowercase letters, and proper spacing. In fact, it really doesn't matter what mastery looks like. What matters is that the teachers *agree* on what mastery looks like and that they all use the same criteria. Collaborative team time is so critical because the discussions and resulting agreements of the team when developing these types of rubrics provide clarity and equity for the assessment. In addition to coming to agreement on performance *criteria*, teams must come to agreement on *levels* of performance. When assessing student writing, teachers should use their collaboration time to score student writing samples using teacher-developed rubrics. Collaborative scoring can be hard work. Teachers often look at the same piece of work and come to different conclusions, yet they must agree on what proficiency looks like. The discussions that the teams have on *why* specific pieces of work warrant certain scores on a rubric provide clarity and consistency to the assessment across classrooms. Collaboratively examining student work promotes collective responsibility for student learning (Langer, Colton, & Goff, 2003). Figure 5.7 (page 100) is an example of a preschool motor development rubric.

Purchased Early Childhood Assessments

An assessment system that teacher teams do not create themselves can also guide decisions about a student's learning and program resources. Published early childhood assessment tools are researched and tested and are accepted by stakeholders as a credible source in assessing a student's development. These are the types of tests that may have to be used for accountability purposes. The key to using these assessments is to make sure that they are observational in nature. A checklist assessment would be an appropriate example.

There are a variety of programs available for preschool teachers. The process of choosing the right assessment tool (if you decide to use one) varies for each early childhood program. Some programs require the use of a specific tool, while others feel that a particular assessment tool meets their needs and aligns to their standards. It is important to remember that your assessment must align with your

Motor Development	3	4	5	Data Collection
Demonstrates awareness of personal space	Not yet able to demonstrate awareness of personal space	With support, demonstrates awareness of personal space	Demonstrates awareness of personal space	Observation
Copies shapes	Correctly traces or copies some shapes (one of four)	Correctly copies most shapes (two to three out of four)	Correctly copies all shapes	Work sample
Copies simple representational drawings	With physical assistance, traces or copies simple representational drawings	With modeling, copies simple representational drawings	Copies simple representational drawings	Work sample
Writes first name, capitalizing initial letter only	Not yet able to demonstrate writing of name	With support, traces name or writes some letters with a model	Writes first name, capitalizing initial letter only without model	Work sample
Copies numerals 1–10	Not yet able to demonstrate writing of numbers	Correctly traces or copies some numerals (five of ten numbers)	Correctly copies all numerals	Work sample

FIGURE 5.7: Example of preschool motor development rubric.

instructional goals and approaches. Different types of prepackaged assessments have different purposes. The team should first determine what it is that they want to measure. What specific targets are they looking to assess? Are they looking at letter or number recognition or counting skills, for example?

Once the purpose has been established, the challenge is to identify the best assessment instrument for the team's needs. It may be one that is widely used or an adaptation of a previously used instrument. It is also perfectly fine to use these types of assessment systems as a starting point for your own system that your team develops. Initially at Willow Grove, we used the assessments that came with our reading curriculum, picking and choosing what pieces to use, creating a customized system tailored to our needs.

Some schools and districts adopt specific curricula to use at the preschool level, such as the OWL Literacy Program by Pearson (https://bit.ly/2VO97br) or Creative Curriculum for Preschool by Teaching Strategies (https://teachingstrategies.com/solutions/teach/preschool).

Many of these come with assessment protocols along with instructional materials. Teams can agree to use these assessment materials or portions of them. Most important to remember is that the items or sections teams use must reflect the specific targets that the team has agreed on. Don't waste time assessing knowledge or skills that do not reflect essential standards. Teacher-created assessments are always preferable; after some use of a purchased assessment, educators may find that a teacher-made assessment more appropriately fits their students' needs. However, you do need a starting point, and a purchased assessment may be beneficial for the time being.

Now you understand the why, what, and how of early childhood assessments. They are an important piece of every program that educates young children. The most important things to remember is that observational methods are the most used, and the driving force behind them should be to answer the second critical question of PLCs: How will we know if they have learned it? (DuFour et al., 2016). Now it's time to move on to the third and fourth critical questions. The next chapter will get into more detail about what early childhood teachers can do when their students have not learned it and when they already know it.

Chapter 6

Data and Interventions

Learning is not attained by chance, it must be sought for with ardor and attended to with diligence.

—Abigail Adams

This chapter discusses what educators do after they assess, why they look at data, and what the next steps are. It addresses question number three, What do we do if they have not learned it? and question number four, What do we do if they already know it (DuFour et al., 2016)?

One important milestone on the PLC journey is when teachers shift from making decisions based on opinions, intuition, or whatever is easiest, and instead defer to data to determine if their learning initiatives are making a difference. That's not to say that educators of young children don't need to continue to use their professional judgment to assist them in making informed decisions about their teaching and student learning, but these must be firmly supported by documented data.

In a PLC, the focus becomes outcomes, not intentions. When teachers examine assessment data, they identify student strengths and weaknesses and apply those findings to their practice. When teachers have accurate information, they can act responsibly to provide support for students who struggle and extensions for those who are proficient. Interpreting data and developing teaching and learning hypotheses allow teachers to provide support for their entire class *and* for individual students. So, when you see that a student has not learned the letters of the alphabet, you don't just move on with instruction and hope for the best; you continue to instruct that student until mastery occurs.

The Importance of Data

Teachers need to become data literate. They need to understand how data analysis and data conversations in schools can build shared understanding. It gives them an opportunity to reflect on their practice and attain relevant information about their teaching strengths and weaknesses. Understanding data is a resource to help teachers teach better. It's essential for teachers to develop their ability to gather, interpret, and use multiple data sources effectively to improve student learning. Teachers may have access to state-, district- and schoolwide data as well as student academic data to evaluate. The focus of their efforts should be to examine the data generated by the common formative assessments that they administer to their students. This is a process by which groups of teachers (teacher teams) collaboratively look at assessment results or student work and analyze the learning experiences they have designed for their students and the progress their students have made in their learning. Educators reflect on their own teaching practices, examine their students' learning, and engage in dialogue with peers. Looking at student work and reflecting on data can help teachers determine the effectiveness of their instruction. These conversations are also an opportunity to improve the rubrics teachers have developed to assess student work. Together teachers build understanding and agreement about the consistent use and interpretation of their rubrics by collectively examining student work. This in turn promotes collective responsibility for student learning (Langer et al., 2003).

Many teachers experience data as unfamiliar or even threatening. This is especially true for teachers of young children. Authentic assessment is a cornerstone of evaluating young children and often emerges naturally as part of the process of working with this age group, but collecting and quantifying the results of assessment is not always part of the process and often does not feel natural initially. Many early childhood teachers do not consider data a resource to improve their teaching. Popham (2001) is correct in assuming that most early childhood teachers are not assessment literate. That is, they don't have a comfortable relationship with data. They don't view data as a resource that can help them and their colleagues guide student learning. Many feel that data are just numbers that they are judged by. Many perceive data as a technical field that requires experts to analyze. Some hold that central office staff should be responsible for all data analysis. Teachers feel, reasonably, that they don't have enough time to teach their students, so where will the time come from to look at the data they have collected?

But these perceptions, while understandable, could not be further from the truth. Data arranged with purpose can be easier to examine than you think. Data left to experts to review create a gulf between the data and the decision makers and are not helpful for teachers. Central office staff and experts can furnish data and scrutinize them, but they can't provide teaching strategies or a deep understanding of the needs of individual students and the practices of teachers. Data meetings must be part of the pacing guide. They must be plugged into the school or grade-level calendar at the beginning of the school year.

Teachers should be prepared for these meetings by having their data compiled and ready to share. Time in schools is always available, but we must be mindful of how we use it. Looking at the data is undeniably important, but taking care not to privilege looking at the data over committing to action is also critical. The strategies I offer in this chapter will help make this process more efficient. Time must be carved out of the school day and year for teachers to engage in this process. Most important, looking at student data is a continuous process and not an isolated event. Early childhood teachers must familiarize themselves with the data process, meet about it, and engage in it.

How to Look at Data

In an article by Thomas W. Many (2009), "Three Rules Help Manage Assessment Data," he discusses three important rules that assist teachers in managing data and outlines what needs to be in place to assist teachers when looking at data together. First, data must be easily accessible. They must be at teachers' fingertips, and they need to be timely to be useful. Data need to be available to teachers efficiently and effectively: "Data loses its impact whenever it takes more than 48 hours to return the results to teachers" (Many, 2009).

The first year that we assessed in my school district, we had to send the information to the IT team to format it for us. It took a week. Well, by that time it was useless information, especially at the early childhood level. Instruction had moved forward, and we had to backtrack. Eventually we went on to create our own, in-house data walls, using Google Docs (www.google.com/docs). Using this tool, every teacher inputs his or her own classroom and student information on a shared grade-level document by a specified date. The teachers then discuss the data and student learning immediately after instruction and assessment occur and come up with a plan to support the students who were not successful in their learning. Schools can also explore other technologies that are available to sort, gather, assemble, and store data. MasteryConnect (www.masteryconnect.com) is a good example of software that classroom teachers can use.

Data must be purposefully arranged. The data must be organized in such a way that it is easy for teachers to see trends and outcomes. The format must be complete, accurate, and straightforward. It must be logical and make sense to the teacher teams that are looking at it. Color-coding results is one helpful method, as it clearly identifies areas of success and areas that need improvement. When data are simple and understandable, then the user does not have to be a statistician. The purpose is for teachers to focus on the results and not the format.

Many (2009) concludes his information about managing data by explaining that when all the data are compiled and the team gets together, it is time for public discussion. This can be a very difficult process for some teachers, as they may feel that it puts their students and their teaching results on display. Many teachers take this as a personal reflection of their teaching and possible failures. This is when the culture of trust and collaboration that is the hallmark of a PLC really comes into play. It is important to stress the use of group norms during these discussions. Teachers must remember that they can benefit from the collective wisdom of the group; doing so can sharpen their pedagogy and deepen their content knowledge. You may sit in meetings like this and feel frustrated or embarrassed because the students in your classroom did not perform as well as the students in other classrooms. Sometimes students just need material presented in a different way, with a different style, or by using a different approach. It is not because you are a poor teacher. Remember that PLCs make average teachers good and good teachers great.

Figure 6.1 is an example of a compiled data chart with different shadings to denote different levels of mastery. Teachers have added their classroom data before the meeting so that the document is ready for discussion. This can be done using a shared Google Doc.

Target: Rote counts 1 to 10			
Exceeds Counts beyond 10	**Mastery** Counts to 10	**Developing** Makes two errors	**Not Demonstrating** Makes more than two errors
Ms. Smith		Ms. Jones	Ms. White
Bill A.		Jackson C.	Erin A.
Paxton C.		Dylan E.	Steven B.
Layla G.		Mary F.	Ellie C.
Frank M.		Justin H.	Caen F.
Joey M.		Sean J.	Zarek F.
Tom M.		Anna M.	Jody L.
Sara P.		Robin P.	John O.
Kimberly S.		Pam S.	Billy R.
Lucy S.		Marcus S.	Rafe S.
Moira T.		Sam T.	Joe T.
Derek V.		Josh W.	Shane U.

FIGURE 6.1: Sample data chart—Rote counting to 10.

In figure 6.1, it is easy to see which students need the most help and support (those with light gray boxes), which students need some help (those with wavy-lined boxes), and which students are ready to move forward (those in dotted and diagonally striped boxes). It may also be useful to have Ms. Jones work with the students who need the most help (those in the darkest shaded boxes) as it appears that her students have mastered the target. She should also share her teaching strategies so that her teammates could try them with the students in their classrooms.

A Protocol for Reviewing Data

There are several steps teams need to be aware of when they review data. Following these steps makes for fluid discussions. In their book *Common Formative Assessment*, Bailey and Jakicic (2012) discuss a protocol for reviewing data that helps teachers turn data into accountable information. A good protocol should consist of agreed-on guidelines that promote effective conversations about teaching and learning. Teachers gather data, analyze them, plan a response, and reflect on the assessment.

Gather the Data

You have already achieved the first step in the data review process once you've collected and charted your data. Data need to be recorded target by target and student by student, as individual students may have mastered some but not all the targets during that instructional period. It's also important to keep in mind that early childhood data differ from elementary data. Preschool classrooms may comprise mixed ages. You should always consider what is developmentally appropriate. For example, you would not expect a three-year-old to count to 10, but you can reasonably expect this of a four-year-old. Teachers should come prepared to the data meeting by first reviewing their own classroom data. They should be aware of which of their students have not achieved mastery, which need more help and support, and which would benefit from enrichment. The team can design a simple chart or form that all teachers can use to have the information readily available. At this time, it is not necessary to discuss how they will help students—right now they are simply determining who needs help, specifically.

Analyze the Data

Once they have gathered their data, teachers evaluate the combined data and note, by target, which students need more help, which achieved mastery, and which students exceeded mastery. The team then defers to the data to ascertain if their learning initiatives are making a difference.

This team approach to data collection and preparation shows that the use of data for improving student achievement is a shared effort within the school and district (Boudett & Moody, 2013) and not an individual teacher effort. Examining data this way "helps the team see the big picture of their data" (Bailey & Jakicic, 2017, pp. 82–83). Bailey and Jakicic (2012) recommend looking at the data and asking these questions.

- "Did the same students miss all of the learning targets?"
- "Did a small percentage of students need additional help?"
- "Did a large majority of students not understand a target?"

Teachers can use this information to group students for corrective instruction or enrichment. It is also helpful to determine if there was one teacher who "had significantly better results than the other teachers" (Bailey & Jakicic, 2012, p. 115). That teacher's instructional strategy should be shared, discussed, and used in the follow-up instruction.

Plan a Response to the Data

After analyzing and responding to the data, the team determines how to move forward. Teachers should have conversations on the most effective ways to help students learn. It is not so much about the data but about the dialogue and what (if any) changes need to be made in instruction. Teachers can share their original instructional strategies with one another and hear multiple ways to teach a concept. This type of sharing should be very detailed. Teachers can come to the meeting with specific materials that they may have used for instruction, such as games, supplies, visuals, and so on. They can share their lessons and have critical conversations afterward. This may sound easy, but as teachers, we often think that everyone else uses the same strategies that we use, or we may feel that our way of teaching a concept is not very original or exceptional. Sometimes we even feel that something is valuable simply because we've taught it the same way for a long time and that way seems to work. But you might discover a whole new way of teaching a concept, or that the way you teach something is brand new to one of your peers. These conversations are immeasurably valuable to all teachers.

In their book *Kid by Kid, Skill by Skill: Teaching in a Professional Learning Community at Work*, Robert Eaker and Janel Keating (2015) suggest that when collaborative teams look at student data, they promote higher-level learning for *all* students, as well as for each individual student. The team should look at the data and determine the teacher who had the most success with a specific target. This teacher can work with a small group of students who need the most support and provide corrective instruction. At times it may be necessary to take a look at the students in a particular classroom. There may be a cluster of special education students or students with English as a second language in a class. Discussions should then center around the best way to support the teacher and the students in this classroom with possibly more assistance. It should be easy to look at the data and determine who this is. If it appears to be a large group of students, the answer may be to reteach the target to the whole group.

Depending on the number of students who need more assistance on a specific target, the team can determine if it is necessary to form a small group for further instruction. Small groups can be very beneficial when reteaching a skill or concept. The teacher is better able to observe individual students and their learning while focusing on providing frequent and personalized feedback. Students can be grouped by specific needs; for example, students who could not rote count one to ten could form a group. As early childhood educators, we must always keep in mind what is developmentally appropriate for our students and not move instruction forward until the student is ready. Young children should be met at the developmental stage they are in, and then receive support to reach goals that are challenging and achievable. Regrouping and moving to a different classroom (for purposes of reteaching or corrective instruction) generally work well for older students, but with our youngest learners, it may not always be appropriate to move them between classrooms or teachers. This is something the team can determine.

Reflect on the Assessment

It is always important to reflect on and discuss the assessment questions based on the student results as a whole. At times, there may be a target that was not assessed properly, but the team doesn't discover this until after the assessment. Maybe the technique in assessing was not appropriate, or it was difficult for the students to understand what the assessment asked of them. The team can then make changes to the assessment of that target so that it correctly reflects mastery.

The data meeting is the time to discuss those groups of students, or individual students, who need more time and support to achieve success. Interpreting data and developing learning hypotheses about how to improve student learning allow teachers to identify the strengths and weaknesses of an entire class and of individual students. Teachers should use the data to look for trends, obstacles, positives, and negatives that will engage staff in public discussions which eventually will lead to higher levels of learning for all students. Reeves (2010) describes the process as a treasure hunt in which teachers look for the best practices that they have and learn how to duplicate them in all classrooms with all students. Data conversations are not defensive but encouraging, reinforcing, and innovative. The hypotheses that the team develops from the data are used to implement and eventually modify individual, developmentally appropriate instruction to improve outcomes. Data discussions are not the destination but part of the journey.

Figure 6.2 is a sample of a data team meeting template that you can use or modify to meet the needs of your team. It is important to know the number of students who are above, below, or proficient in each target, but even more important to know who those students are to make sure that *all* students are learning.

Data Team Meeting Template

Team:
Assessment Description:

Targets Assessed	Type of Assessment	Proficiency Expectation

Target 1			
	Number of Students Below Proficiency	Number of Students at Proficiency	Number of Students Above Proficiency
Teacher 1			
Teacher 2			
Teacher 3			
Teacher 4			

Target 2			
	Number of Students Below Proficiency	Number of Students at Proficiency	Number of Students Above Proficiency
Teacher 1			
Teacher 2			
Teacher 3			
Teacher 4			

Data and Interventions

	Target 3		
	Number of Students Below Proficiency	Number of Students at Proficiency	Number of Students Above Proficiency
Teacher 1			
Teacher 2			
Teacher 3			
Teacher 4			
Which students need more time and support?			

Target 1		
	Students Identified for Intervention, Practice, or Enrichment	Planned Instructional Strategy
Additional time and support		
Additional practice		
Enrichment		

Target 2		
	Students Identified for Intervention, Practice, or Enrichment	Planned Instructional Strategy
Additional time and support		
Additional practice		
Enrichment		

Target 3		
	Students Identified for Intervention, Practice, or Enrichment	Planned Instructional Strategy
Additional time and support		
Additional practice		
Enrichment		

FIGURE 6.2: Data team meeting template.

continued →

Which questions need to be reviewed?	
Question Number	**Concern**

Which teaching strategies or pacing issues need to be discussed?	
Strategy or Topic	**Issue of Concern**

Source: Adapted from Bailey & Jakicic, 2012.

How to Provide Support Through Interventions

Once you have analyzed your data and identified students who may need interventions, it's time to bring your attention to the third critical question of a PLC: What do we do when they have not learned it (DuFour et al., 2016)? In PLCs, the best way to answer this question is through response to intervention (RTI).

RTI is a process by which to deliver all students the additional time and support they need *when they need it*:

> RTI's underlying premise is that schools should not delay providing help for struggling students until they fall far enough behind to qualify for special education, but instead should provide timely, targeted, systematic interventions to all students who demonstrate the need. (Buffum, Mattos, & Weber, 2012, p. xiii)

According to Buffum et al. (2018), RTI is commonly visualized as a pyramid that consists of three tiers. The wide bottom of the pyramid is Tier 1: this is the core instruction that all students receive. When students show the need for more support, they receive Tier 2 instruction. Because RTI concentrates on offering support as soon as students need it, fewer students fall so far behind that they need the intensive support of Tier 3 remedial interventions, which form the narrow top of the pyramid.

Because of common misconceptions about the RTI pyramid's relationship to special education, Buffum et al. (2018) offer an alternate view of the traditional pyramid (see figure 6.3).

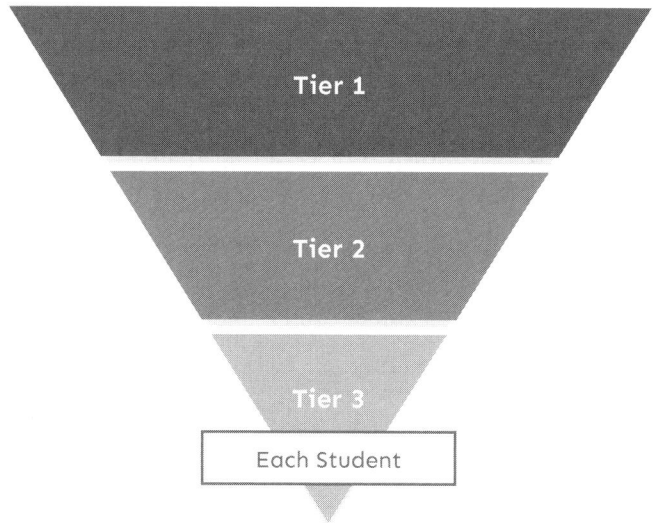

Source: Buffum et al., 2018.

FIGURE 6.3: Inverted RTI at Work pyramid.

Buffum et al. (2018) explain:

> With this approach, the school begins the intervention process assuming that every student is capable of learning at high levels . . . . Because every student does not learn the same way or at the same speed . . . the school builds tiers of additional support to ensure every student's success. The school does not view these tiers as a pathway to traditional special education but instead as an ongoing process to dig deeper into students' individual needs. (p. 19)

Although there is little research focusing on RTI and early childhood, some states and school districts are moving tiered approaches into their preschool programs. The National Professional Development Center on Inclusion (NPDCI, 2012) states, "RTI is a framework that can be used in early childhood to help practitioners connect children's formative assessment results with specific teaching and intervention strategies" (p. 2).

Early childhood RTI is becoming more visible and more aligned with similar practices at the elementary grades. There is a compelling body of evidence that suggests early intervention is the key to students' success and places them in a trajectory for a favorable academic outcome. In fact, RTI is best positioned to begin at the preK level. It complements and extends recommended practices in early childhood education. Instructional strategies and behavioral supports are arranged by tiers from least to most intensive to show the level of adult involvement and time needed to help individual students learn. The specific implementation of RTI at this level may look slightly different, but it's based on the same premise RTI is based on at every level, that "not all children learn the same way and at the same speed" (Bailey & Jakicic, 2012, p. 18).

In early childhood programs, students may not move from classroom to classroom or from teacher to teacher for interventions. Instead, they may receive Tier 2 and Tier 3 instruction in their own classroom setting with additional resources and support from related service providers. Research confirms the importance of this embedded support: "Warm, caring, supportive student-teacher relationships are linked to better school performance and engagement, greater emotional regulation, social competence, and willingness to take on challenges" (Osher, Cantor, Berg, Steyer, & Rose, 2018, as cited in Darling-Hammond, Flook, Cook-Harvey, Barron, & Osher, 2019).

Therefore, I would recommend that students at this young age receive Tier 2 and Tier 3 interventions in the classroom setting or in a comfortable and familiar location with a recognized and predictable adult. Anyone who works with young children knows and understands that they thrive on routine and consistency. Nothing can be scarier for a young child than being trotted off with a strange, new person to a location that he or she is not accustomed to.

The best RTI work at the early childhood level is done at Tier 1. Early educators have the most opportunities to provide a guaranteed and viable core curriculum. Together, as a team, they have already established the essential standards for their students. They achieve implementation of the core curriculum by moving from an environment of incidental learning to an environment of intentional teaching. A solid core curriculum utilizing intentional teaching is the foundation in early childhood programs. Intentional teaching is instruction based on a student's developmental level with a focus on specific learning goals or targets developed by the team. Teachers differentiate, adjust tasks, or do both to match individual student needs. While students still engage in play during center time, the presence of skill-based activities in centers is becoming more evident. Center time consists of clearly defined areas of the classroom grouped by topic, such as blocks, dramatic play, art, and so on. The addition of learning targets for each age level helps identify what these young children should know and be able to do to be successful.

Tier 1 instructional practices that serve as the foundation for RTI are consistent with those widely acknowledged in early childhood classrooms, namely the emphasis on high-quality curriculum and instruction and the importance of early interventions using research-based practices (Buysse & Peisner-Feinberg, 2013). High-quality early childhood programs provide a developmentally appropriate curriculum. Teachers meet students where they are and use teaching practices that are appropriate to a student's age and development. Teachers enable their young students to reach goals that are both challenging and achievable.

When students do not respond to Tier 1 instruction (as determined by the data) they may be considered for supplemental (Tier 2) instruction, in addition to core instruction. This type of targeted intervention for some students provides instructional supports in addition to those provided to all students through the core curriculum and intentional teaching (NPDCI, 2012). The primary purpose of Tier 2 is to reteach academic and behavior standards. Students receive increased opportunities to practice and learn skills that their teachers taught during core instruction. Sessions are short and include alternative activities.

RTI expands the concept of intentional teaching to include targeted interventions for those students who require some help in academic or behavioral areas. Teachers can provide targeted interventions through small-group instruction or embedded instruction. Small groups should be flexible and based on student needs and similar skill levels. Small groups should never consist of more than five students. This type of intentional grouping limits the diversity of need so the teacher can focus his or her instruction on discrete, specific skills. Instruction in these groups is not skill and drill or paper and pencil but consists of engaging activities that promote structured interactions. Students should be talking and listening to each other while engaged in block-building activities, teacher-led games, cooperative drawing, and so on. Students benefit from organized interactions. They develop conversational skills, cooperation skills, and learn how to be fair and share. Teachers can observe the students more closely and provide individualized attention. Preschool teachers can work with a small group while the remainder of the class is engaged in play activities or in other small groups led by support staff.

At Willow Grove, the speech and language therapist led a small group of students who needed assistance in language development while the teacher worked with a group of students who needed additional time and instruction on a specific target. Fremont County School District 25 in Riverton, Wyoming, has made time in its shared schedule for "What I Need" or WIN time for literacy skills (S. Esposito, personal communication, November 12, 2018). Prior to establishing WIN time, team members discussed data and determined which students needed more help and support, which students could be enriched, and which students needed more practice. During WIN time, teachers separated all students into smaller groups and worked with the available learning professionals, including teachers, paraprofessionals, instructional facilitators, and speech teachers on targeted instruction for the clearly and narrowly defined needs of the students. During these times, some students receive enrichment, and some receive reteaching on skills that they need to move forward on the reading continuum. This program has proven successful in improving literacy scores and allowing students to be more prepared for the next grade level.

If a student fails to make improvements when provided with help, then the student requires more intensive support (Tier 3) along with Tier 2 support and the Tier 1 core curriculum. Tier 3 interventions are guided by a site intervention team or problem-solving team, comprising educators who work together as effective problem solvers. Their job is not to determine what is wrong but to identify specific needs that the student has after Tier 2, quantify those needs, and determine how best to meet those needs. Participants on this team may include the principal, RTI coordinator, classroom teacher, special education teacher, literacy and reading specialist, school psychologist, and speech and language therapist. In an early childhood setting, it is not a bad idea to also include an occupational therapist. This diverse group of team members is important when using the problem-solving approach as it relates to young children and their overlapping and sometimes multiple areas of need. They may or may not provide the specific interventions, but they do lead the process of diagnosing, targeting, and monitoring Tier 3.

Tier 3 provides remediation of existing problems and helps prevent more severe learning and behavior issues that may develop later on in school (Buffum et al., 2018). It provides instruction more often, takes more time, has a smaller teacher-student ratio, and is more aligned with individual student needs. Highly trained professionals direct the work of Tier 3 (Buffum et al., 2012). Their research is clear that interventions at this level are more effective when provided by the most highly trained staff in a student's area of need.

Tier 3 offers intensive interventions on essential prerequisite skills. Students enter preschool with a wide range of skills. Many come prepared and ready to learn, yet some do not. These young children may be less advanced than their peers in their acquisition of critical early learning skills (for example, social and behavioral, early literacy, and language skills). Students may be behind in acquiring these skills for a variety of reasons (for example, they are English learners, lack exposure to or experience with print language, exhibit speech-language delays, or have other learning difficulties). These low-performing students benefit most from language and early literacy intervention that is focused on a few priority skills (essential skills), is systematic and individualized, and includes more explicit and comprehensive instruction. Teachers adapt the curriculum using best practices to meet the needs of students who require Tier 3 support.

It is important to remember that interventions don't remove responsibility for student learning from the classroom teacher and support staff but expand the responsibility to all teachers and support staff throughout the building. When teachers and staff become aware of what their students know and are capable of, then they can make a difference. You can use the template in figure 6.4 to record your conversations about individual students.

Individual Problem-Solving Discussion Guide

This tool can be used to focus team discussion related to student progress for learners who are IEP eligible as well as those participating in general education interventions.

Student:	Grade:
Teacher:	Date of Discussion:
Content Area of Focus:	Data Review Date:

Describe the student's present levels in this content area.
(Include normative data, goal-specific data, and progress-monitoring data.)

Relative to this student in this content or skill area:

1. What do we want the student to know and be able to do?

2. How will we know when the student has mastered this skill or these skills? What results will prove this to us? Use specific data indicators.

3. What do we need to know more about in order to help this student meet the targets in questions 1 and 2? What diagnostic tools are available?

4. What will we do instructionally to make sure the student meets the targets listed in questions 1 and 2?

Source: Adapted from Friziellie et al., 2016.

FIGURE 6.4: Discussion guide for individual students.

Visit **go.SolutionTree.com/PLCbooks** for a free reproducible version of this figure.

The collaborative team has determined what it wants its students to know and be able to do. It has worked out a system to respond if students have not learned it. What about the students who have already learned it? Buffum et al. (2012) remind us, "Some consideration should be given, in advance, to how the team might provide meaningful enrichment and extension for those students who demonstrate that they have already mastered these same standards" (p. 54).

Once you have analyzed your data, you may learn that there are some students who have "already learned it" (question four; DuFour et al., 2016). These students may already be proficient in the area that you are assessing and need to either move to the next level or receive enrichment. You must think of these students in much the same way that you think of students in need of more time and support. That is, you can't just do more of the same stuff. If the goal is for your students to be able to verbally recite numbers from one to ten before they enter kindergarten, then the next step would be to count from one to twenty. Extending students' learning means to deepen their knowledge and skills in the core curriculum. A good question to ask yourself when extending a student's learning is, "What can I add to this activity?" Maybe it's supplementing the block area in the classroom with paper and pencil to make street signs, or it might mean asking questions to develop higher-level-thinking skills. This would be a great conversation for a team meeting.

Ensuring that *all* students achieve to high levels is a schoolwide effort. It may not be possible for one teacher alone in his or her classroom to achieve the level of support a student may need. Teachers must analyze data and provide interventions. It requires the total school staff to take responsibility for student success. This level of work may be difficult, but it is well worth it.

CONCLUSION

It is my hope that after reading this book, you will have come to understand and appreciate the bigger implications of your work with young children and how the PLC process can support your work. You can see your classroom as the foundation of the education system. Well-established research continues to emphasize the importance of early childhood education as an essential building block of a student's future success. In her research, child and family policy expert Julia Isaacs (2012) notes that children who attend preschool are more likely to be school-ready than other children and experience better life outcomes. Your program will have a direct effect on the adults these students become, so you should make it the best program around. When you adopt the concepts and begin utilizing the practices of a PLC, you are committing to providing the best education to *all* students.

Your classroom and your teaching are the foundations of a student's education. Your classroom is the place where you can establish a love of learning that lasts a lifetime. Most important, you give your young students the opportunity to achieve success now *and* in the future. Research proves that effective professional learning communities that focus on teaching and learning will yield high dividends in student achievement (Vescio & Adams, 2008). Don't underestimate your value as an integral part of the school system. Don't be left out.

It is also my hope that you will see that becoming a PLC may feel like a complicated process, but one well worth undergoing. It is a long and winding journey, and it doesn't happen overnight—it's part of a sustained process. Your initial progress may be slow, and some of your strategies may fail, but stick with it. You and your team members may become anxious and frustrated when you don't see immediate results; remember that it takes time for a fundamental shift to occur in a school's operation. It is okay to make mistakes and learn from your mistakes. Re-evaluate old beliefs and try new strategies. If you continue to engage in ongoing dialogue about values and beliefs, keep building your capacity to learn, and trust one another, you are on the right track. You, the teacher, drive the work of PLCs. Changing old beliefs and cultures does not happen immediately.

So, where does one begin? It seems like a lot of work. When can we do all of this? How do we get everyone on board? I am sure that you have many more questions and concerns, but first and foremost you probably wonder, How do we start? At Willow Grove, we started with a simple alphabet letter recognition assessment. We gathered as a team and determined exactly what this assessment would look like, how we would administer it, who would give the assessment, and when it would be done. We also decided when to look at our data as a team. As I stated previously, we were pleasantly surprised at how well our students did. This then led us to ask, "What do we want our students to know and be able to do before they move to the next level?" We came to realize that we weren't very clear and together on that, so our focus became student learning and from then on, we asked the preceding question every single day.

Where you begin the process is totally up to your school, district, or team. In KCSD 96, we began with assessments and then collected the data and looked for meaning in them. I personally feel that a good place to start may be with the process of determining what the essential standards are for your early childhood curriculum. In order to do this, you must establish the teams that will do the work. Who will be on the team, when will they meet, and who will lead the discussions? You may be surprised at what your colleagues feel is important. My suggestion is to take one area of learning and go for it. Mathematics is a good place to start. It is easier and offers more concrete targets than literacy. Use the protocol in chapter 5 (page 87) to help organize the process. The goal is to get clarity, as a team, on what is essential for your young students.

One of the biggest keys to improving early childhood programs is to ensure that all teachers are clear on the learning that is to take place in their classrooms and what success looks like for that learning. No matter who a student's teacher is, that student must have access to a guaranteed and viable curriculum developed by the teachers themselves. Educators must be clear on what they want their students to know and be able to do, and they must make these determinations as a team and agree on their decisions. In order to do this, collaborative teams should form, and these teams must have the time to do the work. You may already have teams, but they might not be receiving consistent and reliable times and opportunities to do the work. By working collaboratively, teachers gain clarity and become crystal clear on what they want their students to know and be able to do.

Conclusion

So, start doing something. Make no more excuses. Begin to make changes, even if they are small. It is your moral obligation as a teacher to do the work no matter how hard it is. If it's too hard, it may be a matter of just working smarter. You need to commit to making significant and lasting changes, because when you as a teacher truly believe that *all* students can learn, they do. Every student in every school deserves our best efforts every day, and so we give each one the best learning experience we can. Remember that important child of yours? Think about what you would want for him or her. These young children are all important, and they are depending on you.

REFERENCES AND RESOURCES

ABCmouse.com. (2013). *ABCmouse.com and the Common Core standards.* Accessed at www.ageoflearning.com/style/standards/abcmouse_common_core_standards.pdf on March 25, 2020.

Adel DeSoto Minburn Community School District. (n.d.). *About our district.* Accessed at www.admschools.org/district-2/about-our-community-2 on January 21, 2020.

Ainsworth, L. (2004). *Power standards: Identifying the standards that matter the most.* Englewood, CO: Advanced Learning Press.

Ainsworth, L. (2010). *Rigorous curriculum design: How to create curricular units of study that align standards, instruction, and assessment.* Englewood, CO: Lead and Learn Press.

Ajayi, L., & Collins-Parks, T. (2016). *Teaching literacy across content areas: Effective strategies that reach all K–12 students in the era of the Common Core State Standards.* Newcastle upon Tyne, England: Cambridge Scholars.

AllThingsPLC. (n.d.a). *Alcott Elementary.* Accessed at https://allthingsplc.info/evidence/details/id,638 on November 22, 2019.

AllThingsPLC. (n.d.b). *Aspen Early Learning Center.* Accessed at https://allthingsplc.info/evidence/details/id,1614 on April 21, 2020.

AllThingsPLC. (n.d.c). *Julia Goldstein Early Childhood Education Center.* Accessed at https://allthingsplc.info/evidence/details/id,1474 on April 28, 2020.

AllThingsPLC. (2016). *Glossary of key terms and concepts.* Accessed at https://allthingsplc.info/files/uploads/Terms.pdf on November 22, 2019.

Bagnato, S. J., & Yeh-Ho, H. (2006). High-stakes testing with preschool children: Violation of professional standards for evidence-based practice in early childhood intervention. *KEDI International Journal of Educational Policy, 3*(1), 23–43.

Bailey, K., & Jakicic, C. (2012). *Common formative assessment: A toolkit for Professional Learning Communities at Work*. Bloomington, IN: Solution Tree Press.

Bailey, K., & Jakicic, C. (2017). *Simplifying common assessment: A guide for Professional Learning Communities at Work*. Bloomington, IN: Solution Tree Press.

Barkley, S. G. (2007). *Tapping into student effort, increasing student achievement*. Buffalo, NY: PLS 3rd Learning.

Barnett, W. S., Brown, K., & Shore, R. (2004, April). The universal vs. targeted debate: Should the United States have preschool for all? *Preschool Policy Matters, 6*. New Brunswick, NJ: National Institute for Early Education Research.

Basileo, L. D. (2016). *Did you know? Your school's PLCs have a major impact*. Accessed at www.learningsciences.com/wp/wp-content/uploads/2018/05/Did-You-Know-Your-School%E2%80%99s-PLCs-Have-an-Outsized-Impact.pdf on April 28, 2020.

Berry, B., Johnson, D., & Montgomery, D. (2005). The power of teacher leadership. *Educational Leadership, 62*(5), 56–60.

Blanton, L. P., & Perez, Y. (2011). Exploring the relationship between special education teachers and professional learning communities: Implications of research for administrators. *Journal of Special Education Leadership, 24*(1), 6–16.

Bolam, R., McMahon, A., Stoll, L., Thomas, S., & Wallace, M. (2005). *Creating and sustaining professional learning communities* (Research Report No. 637). London: University of Bristol.

Boudett, K. P., & Moody, L. (2013). Organizing for collaborative work. In K. P. Boudett, E. A. City, & R. J. Murnane (Eds.), *Data wise: A step-by-step guide to using assessment results to improve teaching and learning* (pp. 11–28). Cambridge, MA: Harvard Education Press.

Bowers, S. (2008). Assessing young children: What's old, what's new, and where are we headed? *Early Childhood News: The Professional Resource for Teachers and Parents*. Accessed at www.earlychildhoodnews.com/earlychildhood/article_view.aspx?ArticleID=210 on January 21, 2020.

Bredekamp, S., & Copple, C. (Eds.). (1997). *Developmentally appropriate practice in early childhood programs* (Rev. ed.). Washington, DC: National Association for the Education of Young Children.

Buffum, A., Mattos, M., & Malone, J. (2018). *Taking action: A handbook for RTI at Work*. Bloomington, IN: Solution Tree Press.

Buffum, A., Mattos, M., & Weber, C. (2009). *Pyramid response to intervention: RTI, professional learning communities, and how to respond when kids don't learn*. Bloomington, IN: Solution Tree Press.

References and Resources

Buffum, A., Mattos, M., & Weber, C. (2012). *Simplifying response to intervention: Four essential guiding principles.* Bloomington, IN: Solution Tree Press.

Buysse, V., & Peisner-Feinberg, E. S. (Eds.). (2013). *Handbook of response to intervention in early childhood.* Baltimore: Brookes.

California Department of Education. (2015). *A developmental continuum from early infancy to kindergarten entry: Preschool comprehensive view for use with preschool-age children.* Accessed at www.desiredresults.us/sites/default/files/docs/forms/DRDP2015PSC_090116.pdf on March 25, 2020.

Caruso, J. J. (2007). *Supervision in early childhood education: A developmental perspective* (3rd ed.). New York: Teachers College Press.

Conzemius, A. E., & O'Neill, J. (2014). *The handbook for SMART school teams: Revitalizing best practices for collaboration* (2nd ed.). Bloomington, IN: Solution Tree Press.

Darling-Hammond, L. (n.d.). *What teachers need and reformers ignore: Time to collaborate* [Blog post]. Accessed at https://edpolicy.stanford.edu/library/blog/757 on January 21, 2020.

Darling-Hammond, L., Flook, L., Cook-Harvey, C., Barron, B., & Osher, D. (2019). Implications for educational practice of the science of learning and development. *Applied Developmental Science, 24*(2), 97–140.

Datnow, A., & Castellano, M. (2000, May). *An "inside" look at success for all: A qualitative study of implementation and teaching and learning.* Baltimore: Center for Research on the Education of Students Placed at Risk. (ERIC Document Reproduction Service No. ED441946)

Diamond, K. E., Justice, L. M., Siegler, R. S., & Snyder, P. A. (2013, July). *Synthesis of IES research on early intervention and early childhood education.* Washington, DC: U.S. Department of Education. Accessed at https://ies.ed.gov/ncser/pubs/20133001/pdf/20133001.pdf on January 7, 2018.

DuFour, R. (1991). *The principal as staff developer.* Bloomington, IN: Solution Tree Press.

DuFour, R. (2004). What is a professional learning community? *Educational Leadership, 61*(8), 6–11.

DuFour, R. (2011). Work together: But only if you want to. *Phi Delta Kappan, 92*(5), 57–61.

DuFour, R. (2015). *In praise of American educators: And how they can become even better.* Bloomington, IN: Solution Tree Press.

DuFour, R., & DuFour, R. (2012). *The school leader's guide to Professional Learning Communities at Work.* Bloomington, IN: Solution Tree Press.

DuFour, R., DuFour, R., & Eaker, R. (2008). *Revisiting Professional Learning Communities at Work: New insights for improving schools.* Bloomington, IN: Solution Tree Press.

DuFour, R., DuFour, R., Eaker, R., & Many, T. (2006). *Learning by doing: A handbook for Professional Learning Communities at Work.* Bloomington, IN: Solution Tree Press.

DuFour, R., DuFour, R., Eaker, R., & Many, T. (2010). *Learning by doing: A handbook for Professional Learning Communities at Work* (2nd ed.). Bloomington, IN: Solution Tree Press.

DuFour, R., DuFour, R., Eaker, R., Many, T. W., & Mattos, M. (2016). *Learning by doing: A handbook for Professional Learning Communities at Work* (3rd ed.). Bloomington, IN: Solution Tree Press.

DuFour, R., & Fullan, M. (2013). *Cultures built to last: Systemic PLCs at Work.* Bloomington, IN: Solution Tree Press.

Dweck, C. S. (2016). *Mindset: The new psychology of success* (Updated ed.). New York: Random House.

Eaker, R., & Keating, J. (2015). *Kid by kid, skill by skill: Teaching in a Professional Learning Community at Work.* Bloomington, IN: Solution Tree Press.

Elmore, R. F. (2004). *School reform from the inside out: Policy, practice, and performance.* Cambridge, MA: Harvard Education Press.

Every Student Succeeds Act of 2015, Pub. L. No. 114-95 § 114 Stat. 1177 (2015–2016).

Ferriter, W. M., Graham, P., & Wight, M. (2013). *Making teamwork meaningful: Leading progress-driven collaboration in a PLC.* Bloomington, IN: Solution Tree Press.

Friedman, A. (2018, March 5). *The long-term effects of ineffective teachers.* Accessed at www.brooklynmathtutors.com/the-long-term-effects-of-ineffective-teachers on April 28, 2020.

Friedman-Krauss, A. H., Barnett, W. S., Weisenfeld, G. G., Kasmin, R., DiCrecchio, N., & Horowitz, M. (2018). *The state of preschool 2017: State preschool yearbook.* New Brunswick, NJ: National Institute for Early Education Research.

Friziellie, H., Schmidt, J. A., & Spiller, J. (2016). *Yes we can! General and special educators collaborating in a professional learning community.* Bloomington, IN: Solution Tree Press.

Fullan, M. (2000). The three stories of education reform. *Phi Delta Kappan, 81*(8), 581–584.

Fullan, M. (2008). *Education for continuous improvement.* Accessed at https://michaelfullan.ca/wp-content/uploads/2016/06/Untitled_Document_21.pdf on March 21, 2020.

Gormley, W. T., Jr., Phillips, D., & Gayer, T. (2008). Preschool programs can boost school readiness. *Science, 320,* 1723–1724. Accessed at http://citeseerx.ist.psu.edu/viewdoc/download?doi=10.1.1.621.4481&rep=rep1&type=pdf on November 15, 2019.

Graham, P., & Ferriter, W. M. (2010). *Building a Professional Learning Community at Work: A guide to the first year.* Bloomington, IN: Solution Tree Press.

Guilfoyle, C. (2013). For college and career success, start with preschool. *Policy Priorities: An Information Brief From ASCD, 19*(4), 1–7.

Gullo, D. F. (2006). Alternative means of assessing children's learning in early childhood classrooms. In B. Spodek & O. N. Saracho (Eds.), *Handbook of research on the education of young children* (2nd ed., pp. 443–455). Mahwah, NJ: Erlbaum.

Gullo, D. F., & Hughes, K. (2011). Reclaiming kindergarten: Part II—Questions about policy. *Early Childhood Education Journal, 38*(6), 393–397.

Guskey, T. (2003). How classroom assessments improve learning. *Educational Leadership, 60*(5), 6–11.

Hamos, J. E., Bergin, K. B., Maki, D. P., Perez, L. C., Prival, J. T., Rainey, D. Y., et al. (2009). Opening the classroom door: Professional learning communities in the math and science partnership program. *Science Educator, 18*(2), 14–24.

Hastings Public Schools. (n.d.). *Homepage.* Accessed at https://hastingspublicschools.org on November 25, 2019.

Helm, J. H., & Gronlund, G. (1999). Linking assessment and teaching in the crucial early years. *Classroom Leadership, 2*(6). Accessed at www.ascd.org/publications/classroom-leadership/mar1999/Linking-Assessment-and-Teaching-in-the-Crucial-Early-Years.aspx on November 15, 2019.

Hollins, E. R., McIntyre, L. R., DeBose, C., Hollins, K. S., & Towner, A. (2004). Promoting a self-sustaining learning community: Investigating an internal model for teacher development. *International Journal of Qualitative Studies in Education, 17*(2), 247–264.

Honawar, V. (2008). Working smarter by working together. *Education Week, 27*(31), 25–27.

HuffPost. (2017, November 27). *The U.S. literacy rate hasn't changed in 10 years.* Accessed at https://huffingtonpost.com/2013/09/06/illiteracy-rate_n_3880355.html on January 8, 2018.

Illinois State Board of Education. (2013, September). *Illinois early learning and development standards for preschool.* Springfield, IL: Author. Accessed at www.isbe.net/documents/early_learning_standards.pdf on December 3, 2018.

Improving Head Start for School Readiness Act of 2007, Pub. L. No. 110–134 § 121 Stat. 1363 (2007).

Individuals With Disabilities Education Improvement Act, 20 U.S.C. §1400 *et. seq.* (2004).

Isaacs, J. B. (2012, March). *Starting school at a disadvantage: The school readiness of poor children.* Washington, DC: Center on Children and Families at Brookings. Accessed at https://brookings.edu/wp-content/uploads/2016/06/0319_school_disadvantage_isaacs.pdf on June 15, 2018.

Jablon, J. R., Dombrow, A. L., & Dichtelmiller, M. (1999). *The power of observation from birth through eight.* Bethesda, MD: Teaching Strategies.

Jakicic, C. (2019). *Teams as action researchers.* Accessed at https://allthingsassessment.info/2019/03/04/action-research/ on March 25, 2020.

Karoly, L. A., Kilburn, M. R., & Cannon, J. S. (2005). *Early childhood interventions: Proven results, future promise.* Santa Monica, CA: RAND.

Kildeer Countryside Community Consolidated School District 96. (n.d.). *About KCSD 96.* Accessed at www.kcsd96.org/about on November 25, 2019.

Kruse, S., Louis, K. S., & Bryk, A. (1994, Spring). Building professional community in schools. *Issues in Restructuring Schools, 6,* 3–6. Accessed at http://dieppestaff.pbworks.com/w/file/fetch/66176267/Professional%20Learning%20communities.pdf on January 21, 2020.

Langer, G. M., Colton, A. B., & Goff, L. S. (2003). *Collaborative analysis of student work: Improving teaching and learning.* Alexandria, VA: Association for Supervision and Curriculum Development.

Lieberman, A. (1995). Restructuring schools: The dynamics of changing practice, structure, and culture. In A. Lieberman (Ed.), *The work of restructuring schools: Building from the ground up* (pp. 1–17). New York: Teachers College Press.

Louis, K. S. (2006). Changing the culture of schools: Professional community, organizational learning and trust. *Journal of School Leadership, 16*(4), 477–489.

Louis, K. S., & Gordon, M. F. (2006). *Aligning student support with achievement goals: The secondary principal's guide.* Thousand Oaks, CA: Corwin Press.

Lumpe, A. T. (2007). Research-based professional development: Teachers engaged in professional learning communities. *Journal of Science Teacher Education, 18*(1), 125–128.

Lyon, G. R., Fletcher, J. M., Shaywitz, S. E., Shaywitz, B. A., Torgesen, J. K., Wood, F. B., et al. (2001). Rethinking learning disabilities. In C. E. Finn Jr., A. J. Rotherham, & C. R. Hokanson Jr. (Eds.), *Rethinking special education for a new century* (pp. 259–287). Washington, DC: Fordham Foundation.

Magnuson, K. A., Ruhm, C., & Waldfogel, J. (2007). Does prekindergarten improve school preparation and performance? *Economics of Education Review, 26*(1), 33–51.

Many, T. W. (2009, July 7). *Three rules help manage assessment data* [Blog post]. Accessed at https://allthingsplc.info/blog/view/53/three-rules-help-manage-assessment-data on November 18, 2019.

Marzano, R. J. (2003). *What works in schools: Translating research into action.* Alexandria, VA: Association for Supervision and Curriculum Development.

Marzano, R. J., Heflebower, T., Hoegh, J. K., Warrick, P. B., & Grift, G. (2016). *Collaborative teams that transform schools: The next steps in PLCs.* Bloomington, IN: Marzano Resources.

Mattos, M., DuFour, R., DuFour, R., Eaker, R., & Many, T. W. (2016). *Concise answers to frequently asked questions about Professional Learning Communities at Work.* Bloomington, IN: Solution Tree Press.

Meloy, B., Gardner, M., & Darling-Hammond, L. (2019). *Untangling the evidence on preschool effectiveness.* Palo Alto, CA: Learning Policy Institute.

Meyer, L. (2016). *Report: High-functioning professional learning communities support student achievement.* Accessed at https://thejournal.com/articles/2016/10/24/report-high-functioning-professional-learning-communities-support-student-achievement.aspx on April 28, 2020.

Mitchell, C., & Sackney, L. (Eds.). (2000). *Profound improvement: Building capacity for a learning community.* Lisse, the Netherlands: Swets & Zeitlinger.

Morrison, G. S. (2017). *Fundamentals of early childhood education* (8th ed.). Boston: Pearson.

National Association for the Education of Young Children & National Association of Early Childhood Specialists in State Departments of Education. (2003, November). *Early childhood curriculum, assessment, and program evaluation: Building an effective, accountable system in programs for children birth through age 8* [Joint position statement]. Accessed at www.naeyc.org/sites/default/files/globally-shared/downloads/PDFs/resources/position-statements/pscape.pdf on March 25, 2020.

National Governors Association Center for Best Practices & Council of Chief State School Officers. (n.d.a). *About the standards.* Accessed at www.corestandards.org/about-the-standards on January 22, 2018.

National Governors Association Center for Best Practices & Council of Chief State School Officers. (n.d.b). *Application to students with disabilities.* Accessed at www.corestandards.org/assets/application-to-students-with-disabilities.pdf on November 19, 2019.

National Governors Association Center for Best Practices & Council of Chief State School Officers. (2010a). *Common Core State Standards for English language arts and literacy in history/social studies, science, and technical subjects.* Washington, DC: Authors. Accessed at www.corestandards.org/assets/CCSSI_ELA%20Standards.pdf on November 22, 2019.

National Governors Association Center for Best Practices & Council of Chief State School Officers. (2010b). *Common Core State Standards for mathematics.* Washington, DC: Authors. Accessed at www.corestandards.org/assets/CCSSI_Math%20Standards.pdf on November 22, 2019.

National Professional Development Center on Inclusion. (2012). *Response to intervention (RTI) in early childhood: Building consensus on the defining features.* Chapel Hill: University of North Carolina, FPG Child Development Institute. Accessed at https://npdci.fpg.unc.edu/sites/npdci.fpg.unc.edu/files/resources/NPDCI-RTI-Concept-Paper-FINAL-2-2012.pdf on March 25, 2020.

Nicholson, L. (2016). *Stressed out: The psychological effects of tests on primary school students.* Accessed at https://theconversation.com/stressed-out-the-psychological-effects-of-tests-on-primary-school-children-58913 on March 25, 2020.

Nilsen, S. (2017). Special education and general education: Coordinated or separated? A study of curriculum planning for pupils with special educational needs. *International Journal of Inclusive Education, 21*(2), 205–217.

Noguera, J., & Noguera, P. (2018). Equity through mutual accountability: Collective capacity building helps educators address the needs of all students. *Learning Professional, 39*(5), 44–52.

Office of Head Start. (2019). *Policy and regulations: The Head Start Program performance standards.* Accessed at www.acf.hhs.gov/ohs/policy on March 25, 2020.

Osher, D., Cantor, P., Berg, J., Steyer, L., & Rose, T. (2018). Drivers of human development: How relationships and context shape learning and development. *Applied Developmental Science, 24*(1), 6–36.

Pacchiano, D., Klein, R., & Hawley, M. S. (2016). *Job-embedded professional learning essential to improving teaching and learning in early education.* Chicago: Ounce of Prevention Fund.

Patankar, A. (2013, February 8). Collective inquiry. *Education Week.* Accessed at http://blogs.edweek.org/edweek/global_learning/2013/02/how_teachers_learn.html on April 28, 2020.

Pfeffer, J., & Sutton, R. I. (2000). *The knowing-doing gap: How smart companies turn knowledge into action.* Boston: Harvard Business School Press.

Popham, W. J. (2001). *The truth about testing: An educator's call to action.* Alexandria, VA: Association for Supervision and Curriculum Development.

Popham, W. J. (2003). *Test better, teach better: The instructional role of assessment.* Alexandria, VA: Association for Supervision and Curriculum Development.

Popham, W. J. (2007). All about accountability: The lowdown on learning progressions. *Educational Leadership, 64*(7), 83–84.

President's Council of Economic Advisors. (2014, December). *The economics of early childhood investments.* Washington, DC: Author. Accessed at https://researchconnections.org/childcare/resources/28828/pdf on November 15, 2019.

President's Council of Economic Advisors. (2015, January). *The economics of early childhood investments.* Washington, DC: Author. Accessed at https://obamawhitehouse.archives.gov/sites/default/files/docs/early_childhood_report_update_final_non-embargo.pdf on August 9, 2018.

Reeves, D. B. (2002). *The leader's guide to standards: A blueprint for educational equity and excellence.* San Francisco: Jossey-Bass.

Reeves, D. B. (2003). *High performance in high poverty schools: 90/90/90 and beyond.* Accessed at http://citeseerx.ist.psu.edu/viewdoc/download?doi=10.1.1.453.2112&rep=rep1&type=pdf on November 18, 2019.

Reeves, D. B. (2010). *Transforming professional development into student results.* Alexandria, VA: Association for Supervision and Curriculum Development.

Reeves, D. B. (2019). *Achieving equity and excellence: Immediate results from the lessons of high-poverty, high-success schools.* Bloomington, IN: Solution Tree Press.

Robbins, T., Stagman, S., & Smith, S. (2012). *Young children at risk: National and state prevalence of risk factors.* New York: National Center for Children in Poverty.

Saluja, G., Scott-Little, C., & Clifford, R. M. (2000). Readiness for school: A survey of state policies and definitions. *Early Childhood Research and Practice, 2*(2), 2–55.

Saphier, J. (2005). *John Adams' promise: How to have good schools for all our children, not just for some.* Acton, MA: Research for Better Teaching.

Sarason, S. B. (1996). *Revisiting "The culture of the school and the problem of change."* New York: Teachers College Press.

Schaumburg School District 54. (n.d.). *Mission.* Accessed at https://sd54.org/resources/mission/ on March 25, 2020.

Schlichte, J., Yssel, N., & Merbler, J. (2005). Pathways to burnout: Case studies in teacher isolation and alienation. *Preventing School Failure: Alternative Education for Children and Youth, 50*(1), 35–40. Accessed at https://doi.org/10.3200/PSFL.50.1.35-40 on March 25, 2020.

Schmoker, M. (2001). *The results fieldbook: Practical strategies from dramatically improved schools.* Alexandria, VA: Association for Supervision and Curriculum Development.

Schmoker, M. (2011). *Focus: Elevating the essentials to radically improve student achievement*. Alexandria, VA: Association for Supervision and Curriculum Development.

Schweinhart, L., Montie, J., Xiang, Z., Barnett, W., Belfield, C., & Nores, M. (2005). *Lifetime effects: The High Scope Perry Preschool study through age 40*. Ypsilanti, MI: High Scope Press.

Scribner, J. P. (1999). Professional development: Untangling the influence of work context on teaching learning. *Educational Administration Quarterly, 35*(2), 238–266.

Shonkoff, J. P., & Phillips, D. A. (Eds.). (2000). *From neurons to neighborhoods: The science of early childhood development*. Washington, DC: National Academies Press.

Smith, A. B. (2014). *School completion/academic achievement outcomes of early childhood education*. Accessed at www.child-encyclopedia.com/school-success/according-experts/school-completionacademic-achievement-outcomes-early-childhood on March 19, 2020.

Snow, K. L. (2006). Measuring school readiness: Conceptual and practical considerations. *Early Education and Development, 17*(1), 7–41.

Solution Tree. (2018). *The handbook for embedded formative assessment*. Bloomington, IN: Solution Tree Press.

Sparks, D. (2013). Strong teams, strong schools: Teacher-to-teacher collaboration creates synergy that benefits students. *Journal of Staff Development, 34*(2), 28–30. Accessed at https://learningforward.org/wp-content/uploads/2013/04/strong-teams-strong-schools.pdf on December 8, 2018.

Stiggins, R. J. (1985). Improving assessment where it means the most: In the classroom. *Educational Leadership, 43*(2), 69–74.

Stiggins, R. J. (2017). *The perfect assessment system*. Alexandria, VA: Association for Supervision and Curriculum Development.

Stoll, L., Bolam, R., McMahon, A. J., Wallace, M., & Thomas, S. M. (2006). Professional learning communities: A review of the literature. *Journal of Educational Change, 7*(4), 221–258.

Teaching Strategies. (n.d.). *Our approach: Our 38 objectives*. Accessed at https://teachingstrategies.com/our-approach/our-38-objectives on April 28, 2020.

Teaching Strategies. (2016). *Alignment of GOLD Objectives for Development and Learning: Birth through third grade with Common Core State Standards*. Accessed at https://teachingstrategies.com/wp-content/uploads/2017/05/Common-Core-State-Standards-to-GOLD-B-3-2016.pdf on March 25, 2020.

Teale, W. H. (1988). Developmentally appropriate assessment of reading and writing in the early childhood classroom. *Elementary School Journal, 89*(2), 172–183.

Thurlow, M. L., Quenemoen, R. F., & Lazarus, S. S. (2016). *Meeting the needs of special education students: Recommendations for the Race to the Top consortia and states.* Accessed at https://nceo.umn.edu/docs/OnlinePubs/Martha_Thurlow-Meeting_the_Needs_of_Special_Education_students.pdf on February 4, 2018.

Timperley, H., & Alton-Lee, A. (2008). Reframing teacher professional learning: An alternative policy approach to strengthening valued outcomes for diverse learners. *Review of Research in Education, 32*(1), 328–369.

Toole, J. C., & Louis, K. S. (2002). The role of professional learning communities in international education. In K. Leithwood & P. Hallinger (Eds.), *Second international handbook of educational leadership and administration: Part 1* (pp. 245–279). Dordrecht, the Netherlands: Kluwer Academic.

Tucker, P. D., & Stronge, J. H. (2005). *Linking teacher evaluation and student learning.* Alexandria, VA: Association for Supervision and Curriculum Development.

Twadell, E. (2016, April 6). *Building trust* [Blog post]. Accessed at https://allthingsplc.info/blog/view/323/building-trust on November 7, 2019.

U.S. Department of Education Office of Special Education and Rehabilitative Services. (2002). *A new era: Revitalizing special education for children and their families.* Washington, DC: Author. Accessed at https://ectacenter.org/~pdfs/calls/2010/earlypartc/revitalizing_special_education.pdf on January 21, 2020.

U.S. Department of Education Office of Special Education and Rehabilitative Services. (2014). *New accountability framework raises the bar for state special education programs.* Accessed at www.ed.gov/news/press-releases/new-accountability-framework-raises-bar-state-special-education-programs on March 25, 2020.

U.S. Department of Health and Human Services & U.S. Department of Education. (2015, September 14). *Policy statement on inclusion of children with disabilities in early childhood programs.* Accessed at www2.ed.gov/policy/speced/guid/earlylearning/joint-statement-full-text.pdf on March 25, 2020.

Vescio, V., Ross, D., & Adams, A. (2008). A review of research on the impact of professional learning communities on teaching practice and student learning. *Teaching and Teacher Education, 24*(1), 80–91.

Wei, R., Darling-Hammond, L., Andree, A., Richardson, N., & Orphanos, S. (2009). *Professional learning in the learning profession: A status report on teacher development in the U.S. and abroad* [Technical report]. Accessed at https://edpolicy.stanford.edu/sites/default/files/publications/professional-learning-learning-profession-status-report-teacher-development-us-and-abroad.pdf on April 28, 2020.

Westheimer, J. (1999). Communities and consequences: An inquiry into ideology and practice in teachers' professional work. *Educational Administration Quarterly, 35*(1), 71–105.

Wiggins, G. (1990, November 2). The case of authentic assessment. *Practical Assessment, Research, & Evaluation, 2*(2). Accessed at https://scholarworks.umass.edu/cgi/viewcontent.cgi?article=1024&context=pare on January 22, 2020.

Wood, D. R. (2007). Professional learning communities: Teachers, knowledge, and knowing. *Theory Into Practice, 46*(4), 281–290.

Workman, S., & Ullrich, R. (2017). *Quality 101: Identifying the core components of a high-quality early childhood program.* Accessed at www.americanprogress.org/issues/earlychildhood/reports/2017/02/13/414939/quality-101-identifying-the-core-components-of-a-high-quality-early-childhood-program/ on March 22, 2020.

Yoshikawa, H., Weiland, C., Brooks-Gunn, J., Burchinal, M. R., Espinosa, L., Gormley, W. T., et al. (2013, October). *Investing in our future: The evidence base on preschool education.* Washington, DC: Society for Research in Child Development.

INDEX

A

ABCmouse, 71
Abecedarian Project, 10–11
achievement gap, 4, 11, 64
action research, 27–28
Adams, A., 15, 71
Adele DeSoto Minburn Community School District, 32
agendas, 65, 66, 67
Alcott Elementary School, 16–17
anecdotal notes, 95–97
Aspen Early Learning Center, 15, 16, 24, 52–55
assessment cycle, 89–90
assessments. *See also* data and interventions
  about, 87–89
  common assessments, 26
  common formative assessments, 90–91, 104
  data, importance of, 104
  Developmental Continuum from Early Infancy to Kindergarten Entry, A (California Department of Education) and, 82
  Dynamic Indicators of Basic Early Literacy Skills (DIBELS) and, 16
  early childhood programs and, 18
  essential standards and, 82
  focus on the right things and, 64
  pacing guides and, 85
  performance assessments, 92, 93, 98
  PLCs and, 2, 25
  in preschool and kindergarten, 82–101
  purchased early childhood assessments, 99–101
  reflecting on the assessment, 109–110
  sample number recognition assessment, 94
  sight words checklists, 95
  targets and, 62
  teacher team-created assessments, 92–99
  why assess early childhood students, 89–91
authentic assessments, 90, 93, 104

B

Bailey, K., 80, 93, 107, 108
"bang for your buck" standards, 80
Basileo, L., 48
behavioral supports, 113, 115, 116
Bolam, R., 71
Boones Mill Elementary School, 35, 36
Bowers, S., 89
Buffum, A., 112–113, 118
building blocks of a PLC. *See* PLC (professional learning communities)

C

capacity building, 42
center time, 114
checklists, 94–95, 96
children with disabilities. *See* students with special needs
classrooms
  configurations of early childhood classrooms, 72–74
  diversity of students in, 11–12
  rules for, 33
  segregation and, 48
collaboration
  big ideas of a PLC and, 18, 22, 23
  challenges of collaboration for early childhood educators, 5–6
  culture of PLCs and, 106
  impact of, 3, 18, 47, 50
  school culture and, 21
collaborative teams. *See also* teams
  about, 37–38
  checklists and, 94
  collective inquiry and, 25
  data, reviewing, 108
  definition of, 47
  for early childhood educators, 47–68
  essential standards, identifying, 77–78
  essential standards, determining, 83
  guaranteed and viable curriculum and, 74
  impact of, 120
  organizing teams, 43–47
  rubrics and, 99
  special education services and, 74
  teacher team-created assessments and, 92
  types of teams, 38–43
collective commitments
  example of, 34, 36
  pillars of a PLC and, 28
  values and, 32, 34
collective inquiry, 25–27
common assessments, 26. *See also* assessments
Common Core State Standards (CCSS), 25, 71, 73, 79, 81
Common Formative Assessment (Bailey and Jakicic), 107
common formative assessments, 90–91, 104. See also assessments
consensus building, 82
Creative Curriculum, 71, 79, 81, 101
cross-school teams, 39, 40, 41. See also collaborative teams; teams
culture
  PLCs and, 106
  of privacy/noninterference, 49
  school culture, 21, 23, 42, 68
  shifting from teaching students to students learning and, 71, 72
curriculum
  assessments, purpose of, 89
  essential standards and, 77
  guaranteed and viable curriculum, 74–77
  purchased early childhood assessments and, 99–101
  shifting from teaching students to students learning and, 69–70
  state standards and, 76
  vertical teams and, 40
curriculum maps, 84. *See also* pacing guides
curriculum teams, 41. *See also* collaborative teams; teams
custodians, 28

D

Darling-Hammond, L., 50
data and interventions
  about, 103
  data and the assessment cycle, 89–90

data team meeting template, 110–112
discussion guide for individual students, 117
focus on the right things and, 64
how to look at data, 105–107
importance of data, 103–105
interventions, providing support through, 112–118
reviewing data, protocol for, 107–110
sample data chart—rote counting to 10, 106
developmental continuum, 82
Diamond, K., 4
disabilities, children with. See students with special needs
disabilities, screening for, 89
discussion guide for individual students, 117
district goals, 34. See also goals
documentation
anecdotal notes, 95–97
checklists, 94–95
observations, 91, 93
rubrics, 98–99
DuFour, R.
on learning, 70, 72
on norms, 66
on PLCs, 21–22
on teams, 40, 47, 49
on values, 32
DuFour, R., 21–22
Dynamic Indicators of Basic Early Literacy Skills (DIBELS), 16

E

Eaker, R., 21–22, 108
early childhood programs
assessments and, 2, 18, 89–91
impact of, 119
importance of, PLCs and the, 3–5
need for high-quality early childhood programs. See need for high-quality early childhood programs
RTI and, 113–116
Edmodo, 46
educators. See teachers
electronic teams, 45–47. See also collaborative teams; teams
endurance and standards, 79
essential skills, 116
essential standards. See also standards
about, 77–78
assessments and, 89, 91
critical questions of a PLC and, 25
definition of, 78
grade-level teams and, 38
guaranteed and viable curriculum and, 76
pacing guides and, 56
pacing the standards, how to, 84–86
protocol for determining, 80–84
sample early childhood essential mathematics standards, 84
what do we want our students to know and be able to do, 78–80
Every Student Succeeds Act (ESSA), 88
evidence, 26, 91
extensions, 118
external evidence, 26

F

fist-to-five activity, 62, 63
focus
focus on learning. See learning, focus on
focus on the right things. See right things, focus on
Fremont County School District 25, 115
Friziellie, H., 73
Fullan, M., 18, 47

G

goals
  example of, Boones Mill Elementary School, 36
  guiding coalition and, 41
  mission statements and, 30
  pillars of a PLC and, 29, 34–35
  PLCs and, 21
Google Docs, 105
Google Drive, 45–46
Google Hangouts, 45
GoToMeeting, 45
grade-level teams, 38–40, 82. *See also* collaborative teams; teams
groups, 98, 109, 115
growth mindset, 74
guaranteed and viable curriculum, 74–77, 114
guiding coalition
  collective commitments and, 34
  leadership teams and, 41
  mission statements and, 29
  vision and, 32
Gullo, D., 88
Guskey, T., 91

H

Hastings Public Schools, 30
Head Start, 77, 81, 88
Hughes, K., 88

I

IEP goals, 35, 73–74, 92. *See also* goals
Illinois Early Learning and Development Standards, 25, 80
illiteracy, impact of, 12–13
Improving Head Start for School Readiness Act, 88
Individuals with Disabilities Education Improvement Act (IDEA), 13–14
instructional calendars, 84. *See also* pacing guides
instructional strategies
  action research and, 27–28
  assessments and, 89, 91
  collective inquiry and, 25–27
  data, reviewing, 108–109
  RTI and, 113
intentional teaching, 114, 115
internal evidence, 26
intervention teams, 42–43, 116. *See also* collaborative teams; teams
interventions. *See also* data and interventions
  impact of, 4
  providing support through, 112–118
introduction
  about, 1–3
  about this book, 6–7
  challenges of collaboration for early childhood educators, 5–6
  PLCs and the importance of effective early childhood programs, 3–5
inverted RTI at Work pyramid, 113
Isaacs, J., 119
isolation, tradition of, 47–48, 49

J

Jakicic, C., 80, 93, 107, 108
job-alike teams, 39, 41. *See also* collaborative teams; teams
job-embedded professional learning, 3
Julia Goldstein Early Childhood Education Center, 15
Justice, L., 4

K

Keating, J., 108
Kid by Kid, Skill by Skill: Teaching in a Professional Learning

Community at Work (Eaker and Keating), 108
Kildeer Countryside Community Consolidated School District 96 (KCSD 96). *See also* Willow Grove Kindergarten and Early Childhood Center
   collective commitments and, 34
   curriculum teams and, 41
   meetings and, 51
   as a PLC, 120
   schedules and, 62
kindergarten programs, assessments in, 82–101
kindergarten readiness, 12, 89
kindergarten teachers. *See* teachers

L

leadership teams, 41–42, 50. *See also* collaborative teams; teams
learning, focus on
   about, 69
   big ideas of a PLC and, 18, 22–23
   configurations of early childhood classrooms and, 72–74
   essential standards and, 77–86
   guaranteed and viable curriculum and, 74–77
   school culture and, 42
   shifting from teaching students to students learning, 69–72
Learning by Doing (DuFour), 47, 66, 72
learning progressions, 83
Learning Sciences International research team, 48
learning targets. *See* targets
leverage and standards, 80
Louis, K., 22
Lyon, G., 13

M

Many, T., 21–22, 105, 106
Marzano, R., 17, 75
MasteryConnect, 105
Mattos, M., 21–22, 71, 112
meetings
   collaborative teams and, 50–51
   curriculum teams and, 42
   data meetings, 104–105, 108–110
   data team meeting template, 110–112
   focus on the right things and, 51, 56
   Google Hangouts and, 45
   grade-level teams and, 39
   recording minutes of, 44
   shop and share meetings, 26
   team tools and, 65–68
   vertical teams and, 40
mission/mission statements
   example of, 36
   pillars of a PLC and, 28–30
   PLCs and, 21
   protocol for developing, 31
motor development
   checklists and, 94
   rubric for, 100

N

National Association for the Education of Young Children (NAEYC), 92–93
National Association of Early Childhood Specialists in State Departments of Education (NAECS/SDE), 93
National Institute for Early Childhood Education (NIECE), 4
National Professional Development Center on Inclusion (NPDCI), 113

National Staff Development Council (NSDC), 50
need for high-quality early childhood programs
  about, 9–10
  outcomes for students in early childhood programs, 10–14
  what successful teams in early childhood programs can accomplish, 14–19
New Era: Revitalizing Special Education for Children and Their Families, A (Branstad), 4
Nicholson, L., 88
norms, 65–66, 106
note taker/recorder, 67

O

observations
  anecdotal notes and, 95
  checklists and, 94–95
  essential standards and, 91
  observation recording sheet, 97
  observational assessments, 92–93
  small-group observation form, 98
Opening the World of Learning (OWL), 79, 101

P

pacing guides
  assessments and, 89, 92
  data and, 105
  essential standards and, 84–86
  focus on the right things and, 56
  sample early childhood English language arts pacing guide, 61–62
  sample kindergarten mathematics pacing guide, 56–60
PB Works, 46
performance assessments, 92, 93, 98

Perry Preschool Project, 10–11
pillars of a PLC
  about, 28, 29
  goals, 34–35
  how the pillars work together, 35
  mission, 28–30
  values, 32–34
  vision, 31–32
PLC (professional learning communities)
  about, 1, 21–22
  action research and, 27–28
  assessments and, 2, 88, 90–91
  big ideas of, 18, 22–24
  collaboration and, 37
  collective inquiry and, 25–27
  critical questions of, 24–25
  culture of trust and collaboration and, 106
  data and, 103
  definition of, 21–22
  and early childhood programs, importance of, 3–5
  impact of, 119
  implementation of, 17, 119–120
  isolation and, 48
  pillars of, 28–35
  preK programs and, 14
  teacher participation in, 15, 18, 48, 70
Popham, W., 75, 83, 104
preK programs. *See also* early childhood programs
  classroom segregation and, 48
  impact of, 3
  public schools and, 11
prepackaged assessments, 99–101
prerequisite skills, 116
preschool programs. *See also* early childhood programs
  assessments in, 82–101
  classrooms, configurations of, 73

impact of, 4
participation in PLCs and, 37–38
preschool teachers. *See* teachers
President's Commission on Excellence in Special Education, 4
President's Council of Economic Advisors (PCEA), 11
priority skills, 116
problem-solving teams, 42–43, 116. *See also* collaborative teams; teams
professional development, 3, 43, 50
programs. *See* specific programs
protocol for determining essential standards
   about, 80–81
   step 1, 81
   step 2, 81
   step 3, 81–82
   step 4, 82
   step 5, 82–84
protocol for reviewing data
   analyzing data, 107–108
   gathering data, 107
   planning response to data, 108–109
   reflecting on the assessment, 109–110
purchased early childhood assessments, 99–101

R

readiness and standards, 80
Reeves, D., 18, 25, 79, 109
regrouping, 109
remedial supports/remediation, 13, 116. *See also* interventions; RTI (response to intervention)
results, focus on, 18, 22, 24
Results-Driven Accountability (RDA), 14
reteaching, 109, 115
right things, focus on, 51, 56, 62, 64

Rigorous Curriculum Design (Ainsworth), 78
Ross, D., 15, 71
RTI (response to intervention), 112–116
rubrics, 98–99, 100
rules for a preschool classroom, 33

S

Saphier, J., 4, 18
Sarason, S., 47
schedules. *See also* pacing guides
   example of, 52–55
   meetings, making time for, 50–51
Schmoker, M., 78
school culture, 21, 23, 42, 68
School District 54, 30
school readiness, 12–13, 119
scope and sequence, 69, 84. *See also* pacing guides
Shonkoff, J., 12
shop and share meetings, 26
Siegler, R., 4
sight words checklists, 94–95, 96
Skype, 45
small groups, 98, 109, 115
SMART goals, 34–35. *See also* goals
Smith, A., 4
Snyder, P., 4
Sparks, D., 49
special education services. *See also* students with special needs
   grade-level standards and, 73–74
   problem-solving teams and, 43
   RTI and, 112–113
   students who qualify for, 13–14
special education teachers. *See also* teachers
   isolation and, 47–48
   participation in PLCs and, 37–38
   specialists on teams and, 44–45
specialists on teams, 44–45

standardized testing, 88. *See also* assessments
standards. *See also* essential standards
   critical questions of a PLC and, 25
   electronic teams and, 46
   prioritizing standards, 75
   shifting from teaching students to students learning and, 71
   vertical alignment of, 74–75, 82
State Early Childhood Standards, 79
Stiggins, R., 91
students
   discussion guide for individual students, 117
   outcomes for students in early childhood programs, 10–14
   students learning, shifting from teaching students to, 69–72
   why assess early childhood students, 89–91
students from low-income/poverty, 4, 13
students with special needs. *See also* special education services
   achievement standards and, 75
   classrooms, configurations of early childhood, 73–74
   diversity of in classrooms, 11–12
student-teacher relationships, 114

T

targets. *See also* essential standards
   assessments and, 62, 92
   data, reviewing, 107
   electronic teams and, 46
   pacing guides and, 56, 85
   vertical teams and, 40
teacher team-created assessments
   about, 92–93
   anecdotal notes and, 95–97
   checklists and, 94–95
   rubrics and, 98–99
teachers. *See also* special education teachers
   burn out, 48
   challenges of collaboration for early childhood educators, 5–6
   focus on learning and, 22–23
   impact of, 3, 13, 18–19
   participation in PLCs and, 4–5, 48, 70
teacher-student relationships, 114
teaching students to students learning, shifting from, 69–72
team leaders, role of, 38–39
teams. *See also* collaborative teams
   consensus and, 62
   critical questions of a PLC and, 51
   data, reviewing, 108
   focus on learning and, 23
   impact of, 49–50
   meetings, making time for, 50–51
   roles in, 38–39, 67–68
   rotations for, 44
   size of, 38
   teacher team-created assessments, 92–99
   team configurations, 39
   team goals, 34
   team tools, 64–68
   what successful teams in early childhood programs can accomplish, 14–19
testing, 87–88. *See also* assessments
"Three Rules Help Manage Assessment Data" (Many), 105
Tier 1, 114–115
Tier 2, 115
Tier 3, 116
timekeepers, 67–68
Twaddell, E., 65
twins, separation of, 27–28

U

U.S. Department of Education, 13–14, 73
U.S. Department of Health and Human Services, 73
U.S. Department of Justice, 12

V

values
    example of, Boones Mill Elementary School, 36
    mission statements and, 30
    pillars of a PLC and, 29, 32–34
    PLCs and, 21
vertical teams. *See also* collaborative teams; teams
    essential standards and, 82, 83
    guaranteed and viable curriculum and, 77
    types of teams, 40–41
Vescio, V., 15, 71
vision
    example of, Boones Mill Elementary School, 36
    guiding coalition and, 41
    mission statements and, 30
    pillars of a PLC and, 29, 31–32
    PLCs and, 21

W

what-I-need/WIN time, 115
Willow Grove Kindergarten and Early Childhood Center. *See also* Kildeer Countryside Community Consolidated School District 96 (KCSD 96)
    agendas and, 66
    assessments at, 91, 94–95, 100
    collective inquiry and, 25–26
    essential standards and, 81
    focus on learning and, 21
    mission statements and, 28–29
    norms at, 65
    pillars of a PLC and, 35
    as a PLC, 1, 2–3, 14–15, 120
    RTI and, 115
    standards and, 25
    teams at, 38, 40, 49, 50–51
writing, assessing, 99

Y

Yes We Can (Friziellie), 44
Yoshikawa, H., 3

Z

Zoom, 45

Learning by Doing, Third Edition
Richard DuFour, Rebecca DuFour, Robert Eaker, Thomas W. Many, and Mike Mattos
Discover how to transform your school or district into a high-performing PLC. The third edition of this comprehensive action guide offers new strategies for addressing critical PLC topics, including hiring and retaining new staff, creating team-developed common formative assessments, and more.
BKF746

The Big Book of Tools for Collaborative Teams in a PLC at Work®
William M. Ferriter
Build your team's capacity to become agents of change. Organized around the four critical questions of PLC at Work®, this comprehensive resource provides an explicit structure for learning teams. Access tools and templates for navigating common challenges, developing collective teacher efficacy, and more.
BKF898

What About Us?
Diane Kerr, Tracey A. Hulen, Jacqueline Heller, and Brian K. Butler
Early childhood learning is a critical launchpad for every student's social, emotional, and intellectual growth. With *What About Us?*, discover how to achieve the full potential of preK–2 classrooms through proven best practices aligned to the PLC at Work® process.
BKF941

How to Develop PLCs for Singletons and Small Schools
Aaron Hansen
Ensure singleton teachers feel integrally involved in the PLC process. With this user-friendly guide, you'll discover how small schools, full of singleton teachers who are the only ones in their schools teaching their subject areas, can build successful PLCs.
BKF676

Solution Tree | Press *a division of Solution Tree*

Visit SolutionTree.com or call 800.733.6786 to order.

"Tremendous, tremendous, tremendous!

The speaker made me do some very deep internal reflection about the **PLC process** and the personal responsibility I have in making the school improvement process work **for ALL kids.**"

—Marc Rodriguez, teacher effectiveness coach,
Denver Public Schools, Colorado

PD Services

Our experts draw from decades of research and their own experiences to bring you practical strategies for building and sustaining a high-performing PLC. You can choose from a range of customizable services, from a one-day overview to a multiyear process.

Book your PLC PD today!
888.763.9045

Solution Tree